Steps In Time
The History of Irish Dance in Chicago

Kathleen M. Flanagan

MACATER
P R E S S

Macater Press
PO Box 44305
Madison, Wisconsin 53744

www.macaterpress.com

Printed in the United States of America

Flanagan, Kathleen M.
Steps in time: the history of Irish dance in Chicago

ISBN 978-0-9814924-1-4

Library of Congress Control Number: 2008931225

Cover design: Flying Fish Graphics
Cover photos: front cover, top: J. Ryan, J. McNamara, and J. Coleman, c. 1910, Macater Press
Archives; bottom: Trinity Irish Dancers, reproduced courtesy the Trinity Academy of Irish
Dance. back cover: Irish Village at the World's Columbian Exposition, 1893, Chicago Pub-
lic Library Special Collections and Preservation Division.

Steps in Time

Dedicated to my maternal grandparents,
Jimmy and Rose Rudden Smith,
who taught me my first steps and consistently
nurtured my interest in Irish dancing.

Contents

Illustrations

Preface

Irish dancing has been a part of my life since childhood, learning my first steps from my grandfather in the kitchen after our evening meal. At age ten, when I finally started formal lessons with Pat Roche, traveling to classes became a challenge since by this time my family had moved to a very northern suburb of Chicago. But my interest in Irish dance always kept me involved. Similarly, after my marriage when I moved to a small town in Minnesota, my interest in Irish dance prompted me to start an Irish dance school in this basically Polish, German, and Norwegian town. In 1976 I joined a group of teachers in Chicago to take the T.C.R.G. exam in order to become certified by the Irish Dancing Commission. I continue teaching to this day, doing "evangelization work," attempting to spread Irish culture in southeastern Minnesota.

As I pursued further academic degrees, I started researching the history of Irish dance as part of my program of study. At that point I was concerned because I felt the young Chicago dancers were not aware of, nor able to appreciate, all those who had gone before, those who had laid the foundation that provided them with the opportunity to participate in this cultural expression. I also realized that many of those "pioneers" were aging and soon their stories would not be available.

In 1992, long before Irish dance became an international phenomenon, the first phase of my research began. Much time was spent in Chicago interviewing teachers, participants, and promoters of events. I was able to spend many hours, over several years, interviewing Pat Roche, a key contributor to the development of Irish dance in Chicago. Additionally, since little had been written on Irish dance, my research focused on primary sources: newspaper articles, event programs, and the like. The *Chicago Citizen*, a weekly Irish newspaper printed from 1882-1928, proved to be an excellent source for information. A short-lived newspaper, *The American Gael* published in the late 1930s, provided additional material. Many neighborhood newspapers, such as *The Garfieldian, The Southtown Economist,* and *The Calumet Index* were helpful, but, unfortunately, newspapers from other largely Irish neighborhoods, such as the "back of the yards," were not available.

In 2006, after Irish dance had become a part of American popular culture, I again took up my research in order to focus on Chicago during the last half of the twentieth century. For information about these more recent years, early editions of the *Irish American News* and *The Chicago Tribune* archives were consulted, and many additional interviews were conducted.

Over the last century many people played an active role in promoting and preserving Irish dance in the Chicago area—all those who worked behind the scenes, who transported dancers and musicians, organized and supported fund raising events, opened their homes for lessons, worked on feis committees—all those people are a part of this history, even if not identified by name. Our thanks go out to all those people.

As I hope to show, the city of Chicago has a proud history of Irish dance that will certainly continue to thrive in the years to come and will continue to provide research opportunities for future historians.

Acknowledgments

As with any significant project, there are many people who helped in the process of completing this book. My thanks go to my advisors Dr. William H. A. Williams and Dr. Mary Sheerin who encouraged and challenged me during the early years of my research, the staff at the Abraham Lincoln Presidential Library for their efforts in duplicating photos, Chicago's Joseph Cardinal Bernardin Archives and Record Center, and the staff at the Chicago Public Library and Saint Mary's University Library for their continued assistance. Others who provided leads and suggestions during the beginning stages of my research include Jim Rogers, Marion Casey, John Corrigan, and Ellen Skerret. My appreciation goes to Cliff Carlson at the *Irish American News* for trusting me with archival copies of the paper; Peig Reid, Tom Boyle, and Brian Donovan at the Irish American Heritage Center Library and Archives; and all the scores of people who welcomed me into their homes to share with me their memories and stories of Irish dance. Also, I would like to thank Morris Meyer for having the vision of starting a press to publish Irish dance research, and for encouraging me to publish my work.

My appreciation to Dr. John Cullinane for sharing with me his vast knowledge, incredible resources, and love of Irish dance. John encouraged and assisted me throughout this project. Irish dance scholarship owes a great deal to John as he had the foresight to collect artifacts and to research Irish dance long before anyone else recognized the importance of this endeavor.

Sincere thanks go to my dear friend, colleague, and research associate, Peggy Roche Boyle. Peggy was my Chicago contact person who helped me in multiple ways, but most importantly in networking and arranging numerous interviews. Peggy took part ownership of this project from the beginning and has been an inspiration throughout the process. Finally, thanks to my family, particularly my husband Michael who has assisted me in innumerable ways: proof reading, providing technical support, and, most of all, putting up with me and all my "Irish dancing stuff" for these past thirty-eight years.

Chapter Three first appeared under the title "'Dance and Song of the Gael': Pat Roche and Irish Dance in Chicago, 1933-1953," *New Hibernia Review* 4.4 (2000).

Introduction

Historyans is like doctors. They are always lookin' f'r symptoms. Those iv them that writes about their own times examines th' tongue an' feels th' pulse an' makes a wrong dygnosis. Th' other kind iv histhry is a post-mortem examination. It tells ye what a counthry died iv. But I'd like to know what it lived iv.

—Finley Peter Dunne, *Observations by Mr. Dooley,* 1902

With the enthusiastic reception of *Riverdance,* originally pre-sented as a seven-minute interval in the 1994 Eurovision Song Contest, Irish dancing became an internationally popular en-tertainment quite literally overnight. Entrepreneurs and artists were quick to follow this success by devising the full stage productions of *Riverdance* and *Lord of the Dance* and enthralling audiences world-wide. Like most overnight sensations, the newly discovered phenomenon of Irish dancing was, of course, not new at all. With deep cultural roots, dancing has been on the Irish-American landscape in Chicago for over a century. Since the 1980s the Trinity Irish Dance Company had been producing exciting, bold, innovative works, while Michael Flatley, star of the popular stage show hits and a Chicago native, had amazed local audiences since the 1970s.

These accomplishments are the fruits of a rich history. In America today the Irish as an ethnic group have come of age. However this devel-opmental process has not been without its bumps and bruises. As Lawrence J. McCaffrey suggests, the Irish were the "pioneers of the Amer-ican urban ghetto."[1] He explains that "In their efforts to overcome hate and discrimination and to achieve respectability in the United States, the Irish cultivated ethnic pride."[2] Irish dancing was one of the major expres-sions of this ethnic pride that the immigrants cultivated in their quest for a distinct, positive identity. *Steps in Time* provides an overview of the de-velopment and promotion of Irish dance in Chicago starting in 1893 and spanning the entire twentieth century.

Traditionally, Chicago has had a significant Irish population. By 1893, the first wave of Irish immigrants to Chicago and their descendants had established themselves politically and economically in the city. As Joseph O'Grady points out,

> America no longer despised them, but rather gave them the chance to achieve the better life they sought. They were, in effect, becoming respectable, not as individuals and exceptions to the rule, but as a group and as the rule.[3]

The year 1893 is significant in this story for two particular reasons. In Chicago the Columbian Exposition was underway, while in Ireland the Gaelic League had been founded. Both events had a profound effect on the Irish community in Chicago and specifically on the development and promotion of traditional Irish music and dance.

Presently, Irish dance is thriving in Chicago. There are over twenty different Irish dancing schools located throughout the metropolitan area with thousands of young people taking dance lessons, participating in competitions, and performing. But the teaching and performance of Irish dance in Chicago, as exciting and comprehensive as it is, does not have a well-documented past. No one has chronicled the development of this cultural expression. Many of the individuals who played a significant part in its promotion are aging and dying, their stories being buried with their memories. Many of the programs, photographs, costumes, and other artifacts that were part of this heritage have either been forgotten in attics or already discarded as irrelevant souvenirs.

There has been little research done on the social history of the Irish in America, and even less on Chicago in particular. Those studies that have been done on the Irish in Chicago have centered on the topics of literature, politics, and the Catholic Church. As Andrew Greeley wryly asserts,

> until the historians of the American Irish abandon their concern with politicians, writers, entertainers, and bishops and try to put together a social history of the Irish in the last half of the nineteenth and the first half of the twentieth centuries, we will have to rely on storytellers and retrospective survey data.[4]

He argues that "the academic community has ignored the Irish, refusing to accept them as a significant portion of American society or as an ethnic culture worth scholarly attention."[5] Whether the absence of research on the social and cultural life of Irish-Americans has been deliberate, as Greeley asserts, or not, the fact still remains that there has not been an abundance of research done on these topics. Except for Francis O'Neill's work, the published history of Irish music in Chicago is limited to one study, and until now there has been no significant investigation conducted on Irish dance at all in any geographical location.[6]

Through newspaper articles, display advertisements, programs, photographs, documents, and the memories of those who were involved, the history of Irish dancing in Chicago is chronicled here. It is an attempt to begin the study of this cultural phenomenon, to begin the study of the Irish community in Chicago since, like Mr. Dooley, "I'd like to know what it lived iv."

CHAPTER ONE

First Steps:
The Formation of Irish Dancing
Clubs and Schools, 1893–1909

A t the turn of the twentieth century, Irish dancing in Chicago emerged as an organized activity within a very short period of time between 1893 and 1909. Before 1893 Irish dance performances were sporadic and generally informal and casual. The few performances that had taken place were connected to musical events where dancing served as an entertaining and occasional diversion. But in the space of only fifteen years, Irish dance came into its own with dancing clubs, schools, and instructors active in presenting entertainments that featured dance as the sole or main attraction. From an activity in which only adults participated, it expanded to include and encourage the involvement of the young people in the community.

Before 1893 there were occasional references to traditional Irish dancing in various publications, most consisting of a passing comment that someone had a reputation as a fine dancer.[1] But the major commemorative events and concerts offered specifically by and for the Irish community did not include Irish dancing on their programs at all. A good example of this state of affairs was the March 1893 celebration of the birthday of early nineteenth-century Irish rebel leader, Robert Emmet. At that time in history, Emmet's birthday was as big an Irish holiday as St. Patrick's Day is in the present. And while the event had a variety of musical numbers, there was no dancing. The absence of dance from the 1893 holiday event is significant in pinpointing the date at which the growth and transformation of Chicago Irish dance began.

The World's Columbian Exposition
Two events occurred in 1893 that set the stage for the development of Irish dance in the city. The first was the Chicago World's Columbian Ex-

1. Lady Aberdeen's Irish Village, World's Columbian Exposition, 1893.

position, the largest world's fair ever held to date. The second was the formation, in Ireland, of the Gaelic League. Both events had an enormous impact on the Irish community in Chicago, and specifically on the development and promotion of Irish music and dance. The Columbian Exposition provided the first sustained venue for performances of Irish traditional music and dance. At the same time, on the other side of the Atlantic, the Gaelic League in Ireland was engaged in promoting and reviving traditional performing arts with an evangelical zeal.

Ireland did not have its own building or official exhibit hall on the main fairgrounds of the Columbian Exposition. Instead, the Irish were relegated to the commercially-operated Midway Plaisance, an area comprised of amusements, rides, and exotic novelty exhibits. The Irish on the Midway were represented with not one but two Irish villages. One was organized by Lady Aberdeen, the founder of the Irish Industries Association. [Fig. 1] Her village was located in a very prominent position near

2. Donegal Castle, Mrs. Hart's Irish Village, World's Columbian Exposition, 1893.

the main entrance gate. The exhibit had an entrance based on the Cormac Chapel at the Rock of Cashel, a scale reproduction of Blarney Castle, and cottages meant to recreate Irish village life. Girls were "imported" from Ireland to demonstrate traditional crafts.

The other Irish Village, located farther down on the Midway Plaisance, was developed by Mrs. Ernest Hart, who for years had been a champion in the cause of promoting the Irish crafts industry through the founding of the Donegal Industrial Fund. [Fig. 2] The St. Lawrence Gate of Drogheda formed the entrance to this attraction that included a reproduction of Donegal Castle and its round tower, a plot of genuine Irish soil on which one could stand, and a Wishing Chair. The village included a group of cottages around a village green. "Here, dominated by an intricately carved market cross, villagers, accompanied by an Irish piper, could be found dancing jigs. Inside the cottages Irish peasants were engaged in dyeing, spinning, weaving cloth, making lace, carving Celtic crosses, and

VISIT

DONEGAL CASTLE,

Mrs. Ernest Hart's Irish Village,

Next to Libby's Glassworks,
MIDWAY PLAISANCE.

Ireland's Representative Exhibit of Irish Art, Industry and Antiquity.

Here You May See

The St. Lawrence Gate at Drogheda, The O'Connell Memorial Church, The Giant's Causeway, The Shamrock Garden, The Wishing Chair, Real Irish Soil, Our Gallery of Great Irishmen, The Round Tower, Colossal Bronze Statue of Gladstone, Views of Irish Life.

Visit our Lace, Homespun, Wood-Carving and Kells Embroidery Cottages, and see the villagers at work: Donegal Castle Restaurant, in the ruined keep of the castle, where dainty lunches, dinners and suppers are served at moderate prices—our Specialties are Irish Stew, Stirabout with cream, Carrigeen Moss Blanc Mange, Donegal Chicken Pie; the Refreshment Garden, Thomas Murphy, Manager, where you may get Irish drinks, including Guiness' Dublin Stout, Cantrell & Cochrane's Soda, Dublin Ginger Ale, Powers' Whisky, &c., &c.

Entertainments during the day and evening. Harp solos, Irish ballads, sung by Miss O'Sullivan, from Kerry. Lectures every afternoon at 4 by Mrs. Ernest Hart on the industries of Ireland. Dances on the village green by McSweeny, the Piper, Mackey, the celebrated clog dancer, and the villagers at frequent intervals during the day. Here you may be amused, instructed and entertained all day.

Look out for our Grand Programme on IRISH DAY, Sept. 30. Don't Fail to Visit DONEGAL CASTLE, The Representative Irish Village.

3. Donegal Castle Advertisement.

embroidering."[2] In "Selling National Culture at the World's Columbian Exposition," Neil Harris points out that both Irish villages featured popular entertainment, most notably "the Irish music, the jigs, and the whiskey."[3]

The display advertisement for Mrs. Hart's Irish Village mentions Turlogh McSweeney, the Donegal piper, and Mackay, the dancer. Francis O'Neill, in *Irish Minstrels and Musicians* (1913), dedicates several pages to McSweeney, describing his stay in Chicago and the influence he had on the local Irish musicians. [Fig. 3] Unfortunately, he provides no comments on Mackay or any other dancer who performed at the Donegal Irish Village. In various news clippings about the Irish Villages there are continual references to dancing, but the only dancer mentioned by name is Mackay. Only in a later article published in 1897 was there a reference to Patsy Brannigan who was also a professional dancer at one of the Irish Villages.[4] We know of Patsy Brannigan from a description of Jimmy Lane's dance antics on St. Patrick's Day, 1897. While waiting for the parade to start, Lane heard a band playing an Irish tune and it inspired him to start battering some steps. He also encouraged two other lads to dance a three-hand reel, including Patsy Brannigan who been a performer at the Irish Village of the 1893 Columbian Exposition.[5] The large crowds that gathered to watch this impromptu dancing actually resulted in a delayed start for the parade.[6] What is significant about this 1897 account is not only the recovery of the name of one of the Expo Irish Village performers, but the fact that Brannigan remained in Chicago after the closing of the fair.

The Gaelic League

Meanwhile, in Ireland, the Gaelic League was attempting to rediscover the cultural roots of the country. The goal of the organization was to de-Anglicize Ireland, particularly through the revitalization of the native Gaelic language. However, R.V. Comerford points out that "All evidence suggests that many more people learned to dance reels well than learned to speak Irish well."[7] Indeed, while the League's stated agenda was language revival and the political quest for an independent Ireland, it was the dancing that brought in the crowds and revenue.[8]

One of the League's earliest achievements was the organization of cultural competitions, or *feiseanna* (pl.). The *feis* (sing.), as it was revitalized and conceptualized by the Gaelic League, emphasized language, singing, dancing, storytelling, and essay writing. Irish dance historian John P. Cullinane credits the village of Macroom, Co. Cork, with the organization of the first modern feis in Ireland, August 1899: "The competitions include[d] a written essay on the life of Thomas Davis, recitations, ballads and folk songs, narration of folklore, reel, jig, and hornpipe dancing."[9]

In Chicago the idea of holding a "feis" (but commonly referred to as a "feis ceoil") was adopted from the Gaelic League. At first the term seemed to be used fairly loosely to describe everything from an informal house party that featured a multitude of talented Irish musicians to a large-scale staged public event. Various articles from the Chicago Irish paper, *The Citizen,* from 1900 to 1903 evidence the multiple uses of the term. Unlike in Ireland, the term "feis" as it was being used in Chicago did not imply competition but rather referred to the exhibition of Gaelic performing arts, whether formal or informal.[10]

The development of the feiseanna in Chicago, in regard to both content and timeline, parallels exactly the work of the Gaelic League in Ireland (1893-1910). For whatever reasons, there were some differences in the way in which Chicago translated the feis concept as it was being put into play in Ireland, most notably in the emphasis given to exhibition over competition and the variable degree of formality. But the introduction of the feis ceoil clearly shows the desire of Chicago's Irish community to participate actively in Ireland's Gaelic revival.

The Irish Music Club of Chicago

The Irish Music Club of Chicago, along with the growing prevalence of the "feis ceoil," was certainly instrumental in the development of Irish dance. Formed in 1902, The Irish Music Club's goal (like that of the Gaelic League) was the revival of the ancient music, dances, and songs of Ireland, and its presence in Chicago impacted the cultural life of the Irish community in a profound way. Its roster included Francis O'Neill, the superintendent of police, who is internationally recognized for his efforts and success in collecting and preserving traditional Irish music. Other noted members included James O'Neill who transcribed the collected tunes; Rev. J. K. Fielding, a long-time promoter of Irish events; and John Ennis who acted as an energetic spokesman for the group.

For years a group of Irish music enthusiasts had met monthly at Sgt. James Kerwin's home

> Unhampered by programme or formality. Pipers, fiddlers and fluters galore, with a galaxy of nimble dancers and an abundance of sweet-voiced singers, furnished diversified entertainment the like of which was never known on the shores of Lake Michigan before nor, unfortunately, since.[11]

After awhile, in what Francis O'Neill described as "an evil moment," someone suggested creating a formal organization.[12] Thus the Irish Music Club of Chicago came into existence, growing out of the house parties. O'Neill's negative comment seems to be based on the fact that once the group became structured and involved with finances, pettiness among the members surfaced and the group lost its original innocence. Even though the club prospered and sponsored many fine events, disagreements about the disbursements of funds and other trivial misunderstandings occurred, and musicians began to fall away from the group in 1909. Though the club reorganized and did produce some events after that date, the loss of the quality musicians who had once filled its roster left the club without the vibrancy and effectiveness of previous years.

These early music and dance activities had obviously been successful because by July of 1903, just one year after the founding of the Irish Music Club, John Ennis commented specifically on the increase in the number of people involved with step dancing in the city:

> The great number who participated in the step dancing speaks well for the progress being made in the Irish revival, and the excellence displayed proves that a great many of our people have lately been brushing up their almost forgotten knowledge of the reel, jig, and hornpipe of their boyhood and girlhood days.[13]

The impression given is that those who learned step dancing back in Ireland were now performing these dances more frequently due to the turn-of-the-century renaissance of traditional music. The Irish Music Club's sponsorship of various events—from festivals to balls to feiseanna—cultivated the interest in dancing. Obviously, the more opportunities there were for dancing, the more it became a popular activity in which to engage. "The feis concerts provided showcases for professional and semi-professional performers whose expertise in traditional music or dance were not in demand in music halls or metropolitan theatres."[14]

In the Chicago of 1903, Francis O'Neill said "Dancing was an accomplishment acquired by the majority of young people ... especially those who made any pretense to music."[15] Not surprisingly, then, while describing certain musicians, O'Neill also commented on their dancing ability. For example, in his description of Chicago piper John K. Beatty he says "as a jig and reel dancer he was equal to the best."[16] Elsewhere in the same work, O'Neill proposes that Munster dancers are unequalled:

> In support of this view it may be added that even in our own day in the cosmopolitan city of Chicago, such noted dancers of the old school as Richard Sullivan, Officer Timothy M. Dillon, Sergeants Michael Hartnett and Garret Stack, were born and brought up within a radius of a dozen miles or so of where the Counties of Kerry, Cork, and Limerick come together.[17]

This is an interesting statement in that it locates the region of Ireland where the best dancers came from, as well as listing the names of the best Chicago dancers at the time.

Dancing Clubs and Contests

By 1904, in a testament to the increasing popularity of Irish dancing and the effectiveness of the efforts of the Irish Music Club, organized Irish dance groups came into existence. There were two clubs—the Gaelic Dancing Club and the Feis Ceoil Club. The Gaelic Dancing Club was instructed by Daniel Ryan, a popular dancer and teacher during this era. A critical commentary in a 1904 edition of *Citizen* explains that "The recent arrivals from the Emerald Isle can dance two-steps, polkas, and quadrilles. Very few of them however can creditably dance a hornpipe, reel, or jig."[18] The article continues, stating that Chicago is fortunate to have Dan Ryan, "one of Ireland's best step dancers," willing and able to teach steps.

Ryan immigrated from Kilkenny to Chicago when he was sixteen

4. Dan Ryan's Advertisement, c. 1905.

years old.[19] He worked in the stockyards, but as an entrepreneurial activity he would hold dances at Clifford's Hall located at 63rd and Halsted. An advertisement for the lessons and dances includes a photo of him in the center with time and location placed around the sides. [Fig. 4] A souvenir program from a St. Patrick's Day dance he organized in 1910, also held at Clifford's Hall, lists the variety of dances that would be offered in an evening. Several of them are titled "Quadrilles" accompanied by tunes such as "St. Patrick's Day," or a "selection of Jigs and Reels." Ultimately he bought a tavern at 67th and Halsted that had an attached dance hall. For many years he held his dances there. He did not remain

13

IRISH DAY ON THE LAKE

FIRST GRAND EXCURSION

UNDER AUSPICES OF

The United Irish League of Chicago

CHICAGO TO MILWAUKEE AND RETURN

On S. S. "CHRISTOPHER COLUMBUS"

SUNDAY, JULY 9th, 1905

Entertainment Aboard Boat
by the Irish Choral Society

TICKETS $1.00 FOR THE ROUND TRIP

For Sale by members of the United Irish League and other Irish
organizations. Also at the office of the Chicago Citizen, and
at office of William Dillon, Lawyer, Ashland Block.

EVENTS AND PRIZES

HORNPIPE (for men)—Case of Cream Pure
Rye, donated by John Roche, of Dallemand
& Co., 78 East Lake street.

IRISH JIG (for men)—P. H. Heffron, President
Richelieu Wine Co., 70 East Randolph street,
case of wine.

HORNPIPE (for ladies)—Six-pound package
After Dinner Coffee, donated by H. R. Eagle
& Co., 19 and 21 East Randolph street.

IRISH JIG (for ladies)—Five-pound package
best tea, donated by John Sexton & Co., 16
to 22 State street.

BEST GAELIC SINGER — "Ireland in Pictures," donated by J. S. Hyland & Co., 223-25
Dearborn street.

SMALLEST FOOT (ladies)—Pair of shoes, donated by De Muth & Co., State street and
Jackson boulevard.

Second prize for same—Five-pound box of
candy, donated by C. F. Gunther & Co., 212
State street.

MARRIED MAN WITH LARGEST FAMILY
—Hat, donated by John F. Collins, Madison
and La Salle streets.

Other prizes, which will be announced later,
have been donated by the Washington Shirt
Co., Dearborn and Jackson streets; M. J. Han-
ley & Co., hatters, 127 Dearborn street, and
by Mitchell & Mitchell, hatters, 68 Adams
street.

5. Irish Day on the Lake Advertisement.

in the tavern business or involved with Irish dancing, turning later in life to real estate investments for his livelihood.

Unlike their notable absence in nineteenth-century community activities, by 1905 dance performances were appearing as a common addition at the social events and commemorations sponsored by the Irish community. Typically, programs were held to honor heroes: Thomas Moore's birthday on May 28; O'Donnell's and O'Neill's victories over the English on August 15; the Manchester martyrs, three executed Fenian heroes on November 23; and the important already-mentioned Robert Emmet's birthday on March 04. Of course, St. Patrick's Day was also celebrated, but it definitely shared the stage with all the other celebrations. In addition, various Irish organizations held picnics throughout the summer. Most often the entertainment at these events had centered around instrumental and vocal music. But by 1905 dance was appearing as commonplace. Typical dances performed at these events were the hornpipe, jig, reel, four-hand reel, eight-hand reel, "The Blackbird," "The Job of Journeywork," and the "Humours of Bandon."

Not only were there dance exhibitions, but dance contests also became popular. The prizes were quite different from the medals and trophies awarded at competitions today. In the summer of 1905, the announcement of a dance contest appeared on the advertisement for the "Irish Day on the Lake" sponsored by the United Irish Societies of Chicago. [Fig. 5] The prizes were a case of rye and wine for the men, and a package of coffee and tea for the women. During the same summer the Ancient Order of Hibernians (A.O.H.) also conducted dancing contests at their picnic. John McDonough was awarded a hat and pair of shoes for winning both the jig and hornpipe competitions. At the United Irish Societies picnic on 15 August, McDonough again won first prize, five dollars, for the men's hornpipe while Robert Delaney won a hat as second prize. In the men's jig competition, John McNamara won first prize, a case of whiskey, while E. M. McInerney received a hat for second place. In the women's category, Mary O'Neill won a pair of shoes as first prize in the hornpipe. Mrs. Bender won a ton of hard coal for first place in the married ladies' jig, while Mrs. Doherty won five pounds of tea for placing second.

As mentioned earlier, the term "feis ceoil" was used to describe a variety of events being held in Chicago during those years. In October 1905, the Fourth Annual Feis Ceoil was sponsored by the Irish Music Club. The music and dancing that comprised the program was for exhibition rather than competition. This differed, then, from events of the same name that were being conducted contemporaneously in Ireland solely as competitions. In an article describing the 1905 Feis Ceoil, John McNamara's jig and hornpipe dancing is described. Another gentlemen, James Dever, is mentioned as performing the slip jig. This would be highly unusual in terms of today's competitions where the slip jig is never offered for boys or men nor is it performed by males during dance exhibitions. Another dance on the program, the four-hand reel, was performed by the "Irish Music Club Four." As was too often the case, the dancers who comprised the group were not identified.

Encouraging the Child Dancer

In addition to the new immigrants who actually settled in Chicago, there were also dancers and musicians who passed through town and strongly influenced the local scene. Hugh O'Neill, a dancer and teacher from Limerick, was in Chicago on several occasions during his appearance at the 1904 St. Louis World's Fair. Hugh O'Neill's goal was to have Irish dancing included in the school curriculum in Ireland, and he also suggested that Irish dancing be added to the parochial school curriculum in Chicago and across the United States. This of course did not happen, but whether directly or coincidentally, there was an increase in the number of young people involved in Irish dancing after his visit. Hugh O'Neill definitely had a loyal fan in John Ennis (Irish Music Club) as shown in the glowing poem written by the latter upon O'Neill's departure from Chicago. The poem, which appeared in the 03 December 1904 edition of *Citizen,* is worth quoting in part as a reflection of the then current sentiment:

> At last old Erin's grand old dance is seen throughout the land;
> No more shall Rinnca Fadha by good Irishmen be banned.
> The Anglicized contempt with which we once held jig and reel
> Has been changed to admiration by the skill of Hugh O'Neill.
> For long our matchless dances were neglected and despised,
> And baneful foreign forms of terpsichore were highly prized;
> We imbibed perverted notions that our dance was not genteel,

But those un-Irish fancies were dispelled by Hugh O'Neill.
The waltz and polka now's tabooed from Donegal to Cork;
Once more 'tis "Brandon's Humours" and "The Job of Journeywork,"
"The High Cauled Cap," "The Blackbird" and the dashing eight
    hand reel
Brought back to life and favor by master, Hugh O'Neill.[20]

The need to teach dance to young people became a central community issue. Certainly John Ennis, inspired by O'Neill's agenda, became the loudest voice in calling for the training of children in Irish dance. In 1905 he wrote that

> There seems to be a disposition on the part of our young people to remain passive in this great work of reviving our native songs and dances.... Although we are Americans, there can be no reasons why our Irish pastimes should be relegated to the past leaving them to be preserved only as long as there are people in America who spent their youth on the old sod. There are no dances which bring into play such manly action and feminine grace as ours, and none which are so moral and uplifting.[21]

An article in a 1906 *Citizen,* "Irish Dancing Club," implored that "The teaching of the young will be made a specialty: in them lies the hope of the future and parents should see to it that their children receive a training in the genuine article."[22] The writer continues with disparaging remarks about the "stage style of modern dancing," and demands that "if we want Irish dancing, let us have it right. Let us at least call things by their proper names." Dan Ryan, president of the Irish Dancing Club, was being championed as being

> well known throughout the length and breadth of Chicago as one of the best Irish dancers in the city.... Mr. Ryan has always been thoroughly enthusiastic over the revival of Irish dancing, and he has a splendid, scientific knowledge of the terpsichorean art.[23]

Another dancer's name appears in newspaper stories in 1907. James Coleman, from Co. Tipperary, was cited as winning the jig competition at

6. United Irish Societies Advertisement.

the Clan-na-Gael picnic. Other winners at that event included John Mc-Namara and John Ryan. And by February 1908, "the step dancing of Messrs. Coleman and Ryan and their small students" was noted at a meeting of the Gaelic Society.[24] Apparently, Coleman and Ryan had become the official dance teachers for the Gaelic Society. They and their pupils were also listed on the program for the "Honour to Emmet" Commemoration that took place in March of that year.

Irish Dancing Takes Shape
Demonstrating a positive and successful community response to the exhortations of a few years prior regarding the involvement of children in Irish dancing, the number of students in McNamara's dance classes had astoundingly increased. A newspaper article of 1908 mentions that "fifty boys and girls from the McNamara Gaelic Dancing School" would be performing at the Irish Music Society's Seventh Annual Concert.[25] This is the first mention of an independent and specifically Irish dancing school (as opposed to just a sponsored class) in Chicago. It must have been a development of that year because before that McNamara had been connected with the Irish Music Club. His role as a dance teacher was of great importance since a 1906 list of the club's officers shows John McNamara as holding the office of "Maistir Rinnce," or Dancemaster.[26] Because the Mc-Namara School is first named in 1908 in an article about the Irish Music Club, we might reasonably assume that not only was the school new, but that this may have been their first public appearance under the school name.

By 1908 a distinction was being made between amateur and professional dancers. In an advertisement for the annual United Irish Societies 15 August Celebration and Picnic, separate dance contests for amateurs and professionals were listed on the program. [Fig. 6] It could possibly have been a distinction used to separate competing teachers from competing students. The two dances which were open to professionals were "The Blackbird" and "The Humours of Bandon." Certainly we know that McNamara continued to compete even though he was teaching dance. According to John Cullinane, that was very much the norm at the time, even in Ireland.[27] There were no rules prohibiting teachers from competing, and on occasion teachers would even compete against their own stu-

7. John Ryan, James P. Coleman, and Student.

dents. This is highly significant because, in contemporary Irish dance, teachers are not permitted to compete at all.

With the Gaelic Dancing Association's "grand festival of Gaelic dancing, music, and song" staged in 1909, a definite switch in programming occurred. Formerly, and as previously discussed, public performances centered around instrumental and vocal music, and it was only in 1905 and thereafter that dance numbers began to be included on the program at all. But by 1909 Irish dance was center stage and it was the instrumental and vocal music that had been consigned to secondary roles. This program also introduced the Gaelic Juniors, a group of young dancers from Holy Family Parish. On this program were three distinct dancing schools: Coleman and Ryan's, McNamara's, and the Gaelic Juniors. [Fig. 7]

8. John Ryan, John E. McNamara, and James P. Coleman, c. 1910.

Once again in 1909 the United Irish Societies sponsored dance com-petitions as part of the attractions at their 15 August picnic. Apparently the number of children and adults involved with Irish dance had grown so numerous that the competitions began to divide according to sex and age. There were separate boys' and girls' competitions split into three age groups—under ten years, under sixteen years, and over sixteen. One no-table feature of the program was that after all the dance competitions were completed an exhibition by all the day's medal winners was scheduled. The broad appeal of Irish dancing is reflected in an article that appeared after the event in which the author concluded that "the dancing of the boys and girls this year shows a marked improvement and is a strong indication that Gaelic dancing has taken a strong hold upon the young people."[28]

From 1893 through 1909, Irish dancing grew from informal, casual, and isolated performances to an organized reality comprised of multiple children's Irish dancing schools and competitions. The Hennessey Broth-ers, Daniel Ryan, James Coleman, John Ryan, and John McNamara had all become involved with the teaching of young people. [Fig. 8] By 1909 there were at least three separate dancing schools in Chicago engaged in instruction, competition, and exhibition. This was on a small scale compared to the number of schools, students, and competitions that exist today. But the general outline of contemporary practice was clearly discernible by that date. Interest in and enthusiasm for Irish dancing in Chicago was a reality in 1909 and was, in fact, steadily increasing.

CHAPTER 2

Keeping Time:
Early Performances, Competitions,
and Feiseanna, 1910-1929

In Chicago, the beginning of the second decade of the twentieth century witnessed Irish dance in full bloom. There were several vibrant dance groups and teachers actively involved in its promotion. Internationally, World War I, the Irish Civil War, and the creation of the Irish Free State provided the context within which Irish dancing in Chicago existed.

The Feis as Stage Spectacle

The years 1910-1913 included several major Irish dance events. In May of 1910, a program entitled *The Feis of King Guaire* was held at Orchestra Hall in observance of Thomas Moore's birthday. The event was featured in a beautiful full-page spread in the *Sunday Record Herald*. The article was written and the lay-out designed by Thomas O'Shaughnessy, a noted Chicago artist whose interest and talent in Celtic design is well documented in the many exquisite pieces of his work still on display in Chicago. The beautiful stained glass windows in Chicago's Old St. Patrick's Church, for example, are a testament to his mastery.

O'Shaughnessy designed the costumes that the dancers wore for the pageant. As he described:

> never before in Chicago, or in any other of the world's great centers of Irish population have the ancient dances of the Irish people been danced in the graceful and beautifully flowing garments of the golden age of Ireland, the first centuries of the Christian era.[1]

Detailed descriptions of the costumes and a number of pictures were in-

9. *Feis of King Guaire*, Rinnce Fada.

10. *Feis of King Guaire*: Maria Kennedy and Loretta Kehoe.

RECORD HERALD 22 MAY 1910

11. *Feis of King Guaire,* Dancing the Hornpipe.

cluded in the article. [Figs. 9-11] Interestingly, O'Shaughnessy compared Irish dance to the interlace so prevalent in Celtic design: "the steps of the dance, weaving like the interweaving lines of the decorative art which adorn the architecture and the mantles of the dancers as well."[2] He also made a distinction between the dances "of modest origin" which were based on special occasions in Irish peasant life, and the step dances, "such as the reel, the jig, and the hornpipe and the hop-jig" which are "of more modern origin."[3] He acknowledged that most of the latter dances are well known among Irish-Americans but the former "will be seen for the first time in America in the forthcoming spectacle."[4]

The young dancers who performed were members of the Gaelic Juniors Dancing School. Only a few specialty dances were performed by adults, John McNamara and Martin Hardiman. The sheer number of children involved in the production was impressive. One hundred and fifty youngsters were in the performance, with some pieces including sixty-five and seventy-five young performers. Also, a thirty-two hand reel, performed for "the first time in America," was on the program. The dancing was directed by Professor McNamara.

The following year the Gaelic League presented another "Feis" on May 11 at Orchestra Hall. As described in the *Chicago Daily Tribune,* it did not

12. Emmet Memorial Hall.

seem to be on quite the same theatrical scale as the *Feis of King Guaire.* The event was described as "the first educational gathering of the clans of Chicago since the coming of Douglas Hyde in 1906."[5] The emphasis seemed to be on education rather than entertainment. The costumes were once again under the direction of Thomas O'Shaughnessy. It was described as "Young men and girls dressed in the ancient and medieval costumes will dance, sing, and give exhibitions of sports and customs."[6]

The fact that both of these events were given such elaborate publicity in the mainstream press is significant and illustrates that Irish culture was being celebrated in Chicago and was considered entertainment worthy of the general public. No longer were Irish music and dance confined to the Irish community alone. The chosen venue, Orchestra Hall, also affirms that Irish entertainment was no longer sequestered in the city's Irish neighborhoods but was now center stage in a legitimate and noteworthy music venue. This being said, it was still important for the Irish community to

13. Professors John E. McNamara and Martin J. Hardiman Dancing Team.

have a venue which they could call their own, and in which they could continue to offer cultural programming. With the completion and dedication of Emmet Memorial Hall in October of 1911, this dream was realized. [Fig. 12] The building, located at Taylor Street and Ogden Avenue, was constructed by monies collected over the years by the Ancient Order of Hibernians. As mentioned during the dedication ceremonies, "Here will be a place to properly present the Irish arts, literature and the Irish sciences."[7] Thus, in March of 1912, the celebration of oratory, music, and dancing was held in that auditorium to honor Robert Emmet's birthday.

At all the usual celebrations during 1910-12 dancing exhibitions were given by the pupils of Coleman, Ryan, and McNamara. [Fig. 13] Evidently they were the main, if not the only, instructors during this time period. The Gaelic Juniors Dancing Club of Holy Family Parish continued to provide entertainment at various functions. As noted in the *Citizen,* at the 15 August 1910 celebration, "Professors James J. Coleman, J. J. Ryan and J. McNamara were the high priests of the terpsichorean temple and gave exhibitions of Irish dancing themselves."[8] The young girls who performed

14. Donal O'Connor.

CITIZEN 29 JUNE 1912, ABRAHAM LINCOLN PRESIDENTIAL LIBRARY

were described as wearing "white frocks with green sashes" while the boys "equally neat in their dress, rivalled the girls in their agility and graceful movements."[9] Dance contests for the children continued to be offered and it was reported that "over three hundred dollars in prizes were distributed among the children, it being impossible to say which was better than the other," while in the adult competitions, Dennis O'Leary and Martin Hardiman tied in the men's hornpipe.[10] In April of 1912, McNamara was reported as having over two hundred pupils involved in an entertainment event at Whelan's Hall, 43rd and State Street.[11] Dance was thriving and exhibitions were included in most Irish celebrations.

The First Modern Feis, 1912

Since 1905 dance competitions had continued to be offered at various social events. However, the scope and the level of competition changed significantly during 1912 when Donal O'Connor, a representative of the Gaelic League in Ireland, was sent to Chicago to organize a feis. [Fig. 14] This event was modeled after those that the Gaelic League had successfully revived all over Ireland:

The success of the Gaelic revival has been rightly attributed to the feis. The feis has been the most popular means of creating an interest in the study of the Irish language and because of its success in Ireland the Gaelic League decided to introduce it to America wherever there is a sufficient number of Irishmen to take the matter up."[12]

Feiseanna had already been held in other American cities: Boston, Springfield, and Worchester, Massachusetts; Providence, Rhode Island; and New York. A local committee, which included such familiar Chicago Irish names as Francis O'Neill and Rev. F. K. Fielding, was established to help with the organization.

As in the other locations, the feis featured competitions in Gaelic language (storytelling, conversation, recitation, and singing), instrumental music, dancing, and athletics. This event was centered around competition, and so differed from the previous events, each called a feis, which had been held in Orchestra Hall in 1910 and 1911. Those earlier events, even though each was called "feis," were performances for exhibition rather than competition. As described in the *Tribune,*

> Some of the men will wear saffron hued kilts, the color that was outlawed by an English king in 1446, and others will wear blue, which is the national color of Ireland. The women will be attired in dainty costumes of the fifteenth century.[13]

Avid Gaelic Leaguers dressed in Gaelic garb at League sponsored events, so this costume description applies to a variety of competitors, not necessarily dancers. In this era, Irish dancers did not wear kilts.

Prior to the feis, a letter to the editor appeared in the *Citizen* which described in great detail the attributes needed to be a champion Irish dancer:

> For, make no mistake about it, step dancing is an art and an art in which only the few can hope to excel. Just consider for a moment the qualities, attributes, accomplishments, call them what you will, that go to make the champion dancer. He must have physique and stamina to stand hard work, unusual excellence in bodily proportions; good appearance. He must cultivate correct carriage and

GAELIC MEDALS TO BE
AWARDED AT "FEIS."

15. Feis Medal Designed by Thomas O'Shaughnessy.

graceful bearing. Nature must have endowed him with lower limbs
capable of executing every twist, turn, treble and trick that the
most facile dancers' imagination can regard as possible. Nature
must also have granted him ability to analyze and 'take off' the
best steps of others and to devise new ones of his own. He must
possess unlimited patience for practicing, and he must have some
musical ability or at least a great taste for music.[14]

These same attributes hold true almost a century later. These same char-
acteristics distinguish the exceptional dancer from the average.

As part of the promotion for the event, there was an exhibit of Irish art
industries held at the LaSalle Hotel during the week before the feis. The
exhibit, organized by the Gaelic League in Dublin, included demonstra-
tions in lace making by Bridget O'Quinn, an expert in the art, and work
by Bride Noone, a leather artisan. Also on display were the medals that
would be awarded to the winners at the feis. The medals, designed by
Chicagoan Thomas O'Shaughnessy, were made of solid gold and featured
a celtic cross, intertwining spirals as found in Newgrange, Ireland, and
trinity knots found in Irish decorative design. [Fig. 15]

The feis was held on July 28 at Gaelic Park, located at 47th and California Avenue, and was reported to have attracted five thousand people. Even in 1912, adequate transportation to a venue was a concern to event organizers. Evidently, the street car company did not provide enough extra cars on the route to Gaelic Park, as they had promised, which resulted in hundreds of people waiting on various street corners for street cars to take them to the grounds. "Another thousand persons would have visited the park had there been reasonable accommodation provided on the cars."[15]

There was a bit of a controversy during the feis. The *Chicago Daily Tribune* ran a story the following day entitled, "Stage Irishmen Barred at Fete." According to the article, "Two young Irishmen dressed in knee breeches, green stockings, ragged swallow tail coats and wearing dilapidated hats and green neckerchiefs—they were stage Irishmen—walked up the stairs to the platform where Irish dances were being danced."[16] They were escorted off the stage and told that they could not participate in the competition. Donal O'Connor explained, "We have been fighting this sort of thing for twenty-five years." He continued, "This is no place for burlesque stage Irishmen."[17] The two youths were barred from the contests, but they maintained that, "they were as good Irishmen as any present."[18] For the Gaelic League, authenticity was crucial and anything that did not comply with their vision of authentic Irishness was dismissed outright.

According to the lists of contestants and subsequent winners, the two dancing schools that participated in the feis were the Gaelic Juniors Dancing Club and the Professor John McNamara Dancing School. McNamara not only had students in the feis, but competed himself. This, of course, would not happen at a feis today, since teachers are not allowed to compete, but back then it engendered an enthusiastic response. As reported in the *Citizen:*

> These events created something of a sensation as some of America's best exponents of Irish dancing competed and feeling ran high between the followers of McNamara, Hardiman and Taaffe. The judges, however—Rev. M. O'Sullivan and John D. Curtin—were unanimous in their decisions, pronouncing Prof. McNamara the best in time, style and execution.[19]

The Gaelic Juniors

The Gaelic Juniors Dancing Club continued to flourish. As noted in an article in October of 1912, "Pupils have a double advantage as they not only learn the steps but the correct time also as the music is supplied by the teachers in charge."[20] The teachers were John Ryan and Michael Graham, and they met for lessons on Wednesday evenings at 620 S. Ashland Avenue. In December, the group, along with the Gaelic Junior Choral Club and the Gaelic Junior Orchestra, entertained at a Christmas party for their parents and friends. An article describing the party stated that

> no Irish entertainment in Chicago is worthwhile unless these young people are on the program. They are in demand also at gatherings where the Irish element do not obtain, again and again, they have been invited by members of the Board of Education to give exhibitions of Irish folk dancing at the numerous city parks, and recently at the Child's Welfare Exhibit held at the Andrew Jackson School under the auspices of the Woman's City Club, the Health Department of Chicago and the Schools and Settlements of the 19th Ward.[21]

This account is significant since it points out that Irish dancing was moving outside the Irish community and was appreciated by a larger audience who saw it as a positive influence in the lives of the young people involved. Irish culture was being applauded by members outside the group as something to be emulated rather than as something to be tolerated. Even famed social reformer Jane Addams of Hull House championed the wholesomeness of Irish dancing and the need for it to be taught in the city playgrounds.[22] This account does seem to reflect the self-confident attitude of the Irish community.

Based on the number of young people involved and the variety of Irish cultural activities available, it appears that the Irish community recognized the need to develop an appreciation for Irish culture among its young people. In March 1913, the Gaelic Junior Dramatic Club made its debut with productions of "The Twisting of the Rope" and "The Woman of Wexford." This group joined the other groups of Gaelic Juniors (the dancers, singers, and musicians) who had already gained a fine reputation for their performances. The Gaelic Dancing Association was formed as an umbrella organization for the dancing, choral, instrumental, and dramatic clubs. Mrs. Mary McWhorter, who was involved with the A.O.H. and other Irish activities, was the president. She had also been involved in promoting essay contests in the parochial schools dealing with Irish history. When she declined renomination, James Ryan became the new president.

One young person of whom the Irish community was extremely proud was Selena O'Neill. By the age of eighteen she had already completed a Bachelor of Music degree at the Chicago Musical College. She was a magnificent musician and won first place medals in the violin and piano competitions at the feis in Philadelphia. Even though she was in great demand as a performer, for St. Patrick's Day she chose to perform with the Gaelic Juniors, because she explained that was "where her heart is."[23]

Evidently, Irish dance did attract students who were not Irish. One article described the election of the officers for the Gaelic Dancing Association, all of whom appear to have been youngsters:

> There was no hard feeling shown in the election of Miss Frances Lichter, whom we unanimously elected our president. Miss Frances is a pretty blue-eyed German girl, and, we believe, will be one of the best Irish step-dancers in Chicago.[24]

It seems that this particular organization was different from the organization of the same name described earlier, since there was no mention of the Gaelic Juniors. Also, the other organization had adult officers. This new group was formed to promote Irish dancing on the north side of the city: "it is expected that there will be a class of at least 500 hundred pupils in St. Vincent Parish in a very short time."[25] The instructor for the group was Prof. John McNamara, "who is famous, not in Chicago alone, but all through the country, and as far as the cross-roads in Ireland."[26]

The Gaelic Feis, 1913

During the summer of 1913, the third grand event took place (*The Feis of King Guaire* and the 1912 feis being the first two grand events). The Gaelic League once again sponsored a feis in Chicago. The Tara Feis, as it was being called, was held at Comiskey Park, home of the Chicago White Sox baseball team on 03 August. [Fig. 16] The use of the park (which could ac-

GAELIC FEIS

(Organized by Gaelic League of Ireland and Chicago Gaelic Society)

Comiskey Park
(35th and Wentworth Ave.)

Sunday, August 3rd, 1913

31 Contests

Singing	Violin	Jig
Storytelling	Flute	Reel
Reciting		
Essay Writing	Highland Pipes	Hornpipe
etc., etc.	Irish Pipes	Figure Dances

!!! Prizes from Ireland !!!

Seventh Regt. Band

Football and Hurling

"Tir agus teanga"

Feis Office, 501 Unity Building

16. Gaelic Feis Advertisement.

commodate thirty-five thousand people) was donated by Charles A. Comiskey, the president of the ball club. Once again, Donal O'Connor from Ireland was the chief organizer. [Fig.17] It was mentioned that the entire proceeds of the Feis would be sent to the Gaelic League in Dublin to provide funds for their continued work.[27]

The *Chicago Daily Tribune* featured an article describing the program:

> There are thirty-one contests on the program, including Gaelic singing, story telling, reciting, essay writing, conversation tests for students of Irish, playing on the violin, flute, harp, war pipes, highland pipes, and union pipes, dancing the jig, reel, hornpipe, "Blackbird," "Three Sea Captains," and other old Irish dances besides the four hand and eight hand reels, and jigs.[29]

17. Donal O'Connor.

This account is the first and only time in this era that the "Three Sea Captains," a solo set dance, is mentioned as being performed by Chicago Irish dancers.

The special highlight of the day was Governor Edward Dunne who opened the program with a speech. His daughter, Alice Dunne, danced the highland fling.[29] At this feis, as in later feiseanna in Chicago, several competitions in Scottish dancing were included on the program. In Irish dancing competitions, James Coleman, John J. Ryan, John McNamara, and Martin Hardiman were the principal contestants. The Gaelic Juniors, as well as the John McNamara Dancing School, sent large contingents. It was reported that ten thousand people were in attendance for the event.[30]

The McNamara School

During the next several years, 1914 through 1917, events in Irish dancing are difficult to chronicle because copies of the Irish newspaper covering that era are unavailable. Of course, these years coincide with World War I, so the lack of information on Irish dancing during these years might be related.[31] In 1917, when coverage continues there are several groups which are no longer in the news. The Gaelic Juniors, for example, are not to be found. James Coleman and John Ryan were apparently out of the picture, at least in regard to teaching Irish dance, and

18. Florence Giblin, McNamara School,
St. Patrick's Day, 1918.

Professor John McNamara seemed to be the only instructor in the Chicago area.

Although McNamara spent his youth in Ireland and learned dancing there, he was actually born in the United States, in Galitzen, Pennsylvania in 1874. When he was about six years old, he was taken to Limerick, Ireland. While there, he took lessons from the noted Irish dance teacher, Professor Halpin. In 1902, McNamara arrived in Chicago and immediately became involved with Irish dancing. By 1917, his reputation had spread to the surrounding states. One article talks about his trip with several of his young dancers to Missouri to perform at a picnic. The account of McNamara's dancing performance is testament to the high esteem with which he was regarded:

The artistic exhibitions of Mr. McNamara himself proved him indeed the 'Prince of Dancers,' and he was never in better form. The

19. McNamara School Dancers, St. Patrick's Day, 1918: Lillian Moore,
May Nolan, Mamie Nolan, Catherine McMahon

fact that but very few present had ever seen an Irish jig or hornpipe danced seemed to spur him on to a point of perfection in his performances that could not be surpassed. The grace and ease with which he danced most difficult steps was surely a revelation and won round after round of applause from the spectators who compelled him to respond to numberless encores."[32]

Around St. Patrick's Day, 1917 and 1918, McNamara's pupils are listed as providing the dancing entertainment at all of the performances mentioned. For one of the events, the United Celtic American Societies reception and ball, two hundred of McNamara's dancers were scheduled to perform. [Figs. 18-19] Dance contests were also part of this program. In fact, McNamara himself challenged other dancers to a contest for the American championship, and Tom Hill, who was a noted dancer from New York, was listed as a contender. Along with Hill, top dancers from St.

GAELIC PARK

47th Street and California Avenue

Every Sunday

Afternoon and Evening

ATHLETIC EVENTS
MUSIC — DANCING

Irish Dancing by Prof. McNamara and Pupils

20. Gaelic Park Advertisement.

Louis and Milwaukee were also scheduled to compete against McNamara. In one article, the contender from New York expressed some concern about the selection of judges for the event, since styles of dancing differ in different parts of Ireland and that might influence the decision. He suggested that there be a deliberate attempt to get judges who were originally from various regions in Ireland in order to insure fairness.[33]

Many of the commemorations and celebrations of earlier years were no longer observed. St. Patrick's Day celebrations in March, several gatherings at Gaelic Park during the summer, and the observance of August 15 seemed to be the extent of the social gatherings that featured Irish dancing. When Gaelic Park opened for the season in May 1918, the "usual entertainers were on hand, including Tom Walsh and his orchestra; Adam Tobin, 'King of the Pipers,' who furnishes the music for Professor McNamara and his wonderful pupils."[34] This comment seems to indicate that McNamara and his pupils had been regulars at Gaelic Park for many years. [Fig. 20] Later in the summer, the tenth annual McNamara Day at Gaelic Park was advertised and, in the following summer of 1919, another McNamara Day at Gaelic Park was held. The significant point is that McNamara was involved with providing dancing entertainment and contests at Gaelic Park for many years.

In July of 1918 there was a dance contest with over one hundred young people involved. McNamara publicized that he "would stage a championship contest between his city pupils and out of town contenders, which will include Milwaukee, Elgin, Aurora, Chicago Heights, Hammond, St. Louis, and many other towns."[35] It is not clear whether or not the out of town dancers were McNamara's pupils. However, in the summer of 1919, another article about Gaelic Park mentions "a dance contest in which all of Mr. McNamara's classes will take part, and some of his best dancers from Milwaukee and many other surrounding states will take part in."[36] Evidently, at this point McNamara was teaching outside the Chicago area. In fact a few years later, in 1921, an article specifically states that, "The professor's classes call him not only all over Chicago but also to Hammond, Whiting, Joliet and other nearby cities."[37]

Another interesting development was that in 1918 an old country set dancing contest was held at Gaelic Park for the first time. Up until this time, dance contests were for step dancing or figure dances. Set dances were country dances derived from quadrilles, popular during Napoleonic times. The Irish adapted these continental dances and made them their own. Most people coming from rural Ireland knew sets, even if they did not know step dancing. It is surprising, though, that set dances were included in competition as they had been excluded from competitions in Ireland.[38] Again in the summer of 1919, contests in set dancing were held at Gaelic Park. McNamara also continued to hold step dancing contests among his own students several times each summer. There are not many descriptions of costumes or photos during this time; however, an article about Gaelic Park mentions McNamara's girl step dancers "dressed in pretty green costumes."[39]

The End of an Era

By 1920 some of the Chicago dancers were apparently competing with dancers from other parts of the United States. [Fig. 21] An article appearing in March 1920 described Miss Bernice Mahoney as "the champion Irish girl dancer of the United States."[40] That statement might have been merely an assumption on the part of the writer, based on Miss Mahoney's acknowledged ability. But the same article specifically mentions Thomas Cunningham, "who recently captured three first prizes in dancing at the

MISS OLIVE KELLY AND WILLIAM FERRY, Who Will Dance Jig & Reel Contest at Entertainment and Ball of United Celtic Societies St. Patrick's Night, March 17th, at White City.

21. Olive Kelly and William Ferry, St. Patrick's Day, 1920.

New York Feis, November 23."[41] This statement seems to be based on an actual occurrence rather than mere conjecture. However, most of the competitions held in Chicago were just class competitions among McNamara's pupils, nothing on the scale of the Gaelic League Feiseanna that were held in 1912 and 1913. Similarly, the programs at which dancing was performed were not on the same scale as the *Feis of King Guaire* held at Orchestra Hall in 1910. Irish dance was still a reality, but the number of teachers and the variety and quality of the performances seemed to be dwindling.

In various articles published between 1912 and 1921, several names which would appear later as teachers and/or judges in Irish dance in Chicago appear on the lists of McNamara's dancers, either performing or competing at various events. Names such as Margaret Hayes, Hannah Dalton, Mary Kennedy, Anna Lynch, and Mary Lynch were frequently cited.

During the 1920s there was not much coverage of Irish dancing performances in the press. The *Citizen* became a smaller paper and had few articles on the cultural life of the Chicago Irish community. For instance in 1924, even on St. Patrick's Day, there was not one article that mentioned entertainment in general let alone dancing specifically. Throughout this time period there were a few articles that might mention that Irish dancing would be included at an event, but without any mention of specific names. In 1924, there was an article in the *Citizen* explaining the tradition of the August 15 feast day, Our Lady Day in Harvest, which was celebrated in Ireland. In earlier years, August 15 was celebrated by the Chicago Irish community with more nationalistic spirit, praising military victories over the English. Now the emphasis switched to the religious.[42] The article encouraged the readers to attend the scheduled picnic and participate in this cultural celebration, indicating that attendance was dwindling and that the community needed a push.

The name of another dancing teacher did appear in the *Southtown Economist*, a neighborhood newspaper, in September of 1925. An article about "Ireland's Days," scheduled for Gaelic Park, mentions that: "Pupils of the McNamara dancing school and those from the Paul Dillon academy will entertain the spectators with exhibition of Irish and American dance."[43] This was the first mention of a new teacher and school other than McNamara's, and Paul Dillon's name continues to appear as an Irish dance teacher in Chicago over the next decades.

There is no specific mention of Irish step or figure dancing in the *Citizen* article publicizing the August 15 celebration in 1926. However, in a subsequent article it mentioned that pupils of Miss Margaret Hayes were entered in the dancing contests held at that picnic.[44] This is the first indication that some of McNamara's students were now teaching their own classes.

One short but interesting news note appeared in the *Citizen* in July of 1926. A statement from Elizabeth Burchenal of the American Folk Dance Society, who authored *Rinnce Na Eirann: National Dances of Ireland,* said that her organization "was eager to put Irish group dancing in the forefront of the folk dancing movement in America."[45] This article provides another example of Irish dancing being lauded by those outside the Irish community. Just as in the articles in 1913, Irish dance is commended as a positive and enjoyable pastime.

Even though Irish dancing was most likely being taught and performed during the 1920s, it was certainly not getting the type of news coverage that it did during earlier years. No doubt this situation was due in part to the deteriorated state of the Irish press in Chicago. The *Citizen,* which had been published weekly since the 1880s, finally discontinued publication in the late 1920s after a gradual demise. The void created by the absence of an Irish paper was noticeable. There was also an apparent lack of leadership in Irish organizations. Names from the past—the Irish Music Club, the Gaelic League, the Gaelic Juniors, and the Gaelic Dancing Association—were either no longer in existence or no longer providing the vibrant, enthusiastic leadership and sponsorship of Irish cultural events in Chicago.

When this era began, there were several dance teachers holding classes. Ultimately, McNamara was the lone survivor from that group and seemed to have established a dancing dynasty in Chicago. After suffering with a "lingering illness" for nearly a year, John E. McNamara died on January 20, 1929. His funeral was held at Nativity, his home parish, and he was buried in Mount Olivet Cemetery. In his obituary, printed in *The New World,* it states, "He was considered the most successful teacher of his line in America. He also took part in many contests and won many medals."[46] His death ended an era. He had taught dancing for nearly twenty-six years. But, as mentioned earlier, by the late 1920s, a few new names began to appear as teachers. Paul Dillon, who hailed from County Wexford, and several of McNamara's former students were cited as teaching Irish dance.

Another factor which had some impact on the state of dancing in Chicago was the creation of the Irish Free State. With its creation, the nationalistic fervor which had inspired so many Irish gatherings was quenched. The cause, freedom from British rule, had seemingly been realized. There was a small group who continued to articulate the need for a reunited Ireland, but the real fire of the nationalist movement had been quenched.[47] During the 1930s, there was more rhetoric about the need to reunite Ireland, but the main battle had been won, so for most Irish-Americans, life simply went on.

All the enthusiasm for Irish dancing which had been displayed during the first two decades of the century, seemed to wane during the 1920s. As one source notes:

> Gaelic Park at 47th and California Avenue on the South Side had to be sold to pay past due taxes and the Emmet Memorial Hall, built in 1911 on the city's West Side, became a victim of the wrecker's ball. World War I, the 1920's, and the Depression all took their toll on Irish cultural life. Indeed, immigrants who came to Chicago in the 1930's thought that they were organizing Irish activities for the first time![48]

22. Entertainers from Ireland: Dennis Cox, Violet Danaher,
and Peter Bolton, World's Fair Irish Village, 1934.

CHAPTER 3

Step About:
Chicago Promotes National
Connections, 1930-1952

I rish immigrants who settled in Chicago in the late 1920s and early
1930s were not completely aware of the Irish cultural activity that had
preceded their arrival. Nevertheless, the new immigrants did exhibit
an exuberance and enthusiasm for Irish music and dance, as demonstrated by their support of social and cultural groups. This renewed interest in Irish culture was reinforced by the creation of the Irish Village at
the Century of Progress, the world's fair held in Chicago during 1933 and
1934. Just as was the case with the World's Columbian Exposition of 1893,
the Century of Progress, and more specifically the Irish Village, provided
a sustained venue for Irish music and dance and provided the Irish community with a common point of interest.

The 1933 World's Fair Irish Village
The Irish Village struggled constantly to keep financially afloat. The village, a locally-organized venture, had no official connection with any organization in Ireland. It was conceptualized and initiated by a group of
Irish-American business and civic leaders who imported artifacts and entertainers from Ireland for the Village. As announced in an article in the
New World, the Chicago Catholic archdiocesan newspaper, three performers arrived at the village: Dennis Cox, an accomplished vocalist; Violet Danaher, a champion Irish dancer; and Peter Bolton, another
champion Irish dancer.[1] [Fig. 22]

The organizers of the Irish Village, in the hope of increasing attendance, brought in non-Irish entertainment as well. There was no written
description of the entertainment available, but Pat Roche, who was subsequently involved with the Village, commented:

They brought in sideshows trying to follow on the same "nick" as the Streets of Paris and Sally Rand and all this to get people into the Village, but, see, the Irish weren't interested and the other people who weren't Irish could go across to the English Village or the German Black Forest down the street. Then the sisters came in and they didn't like the way the dancers were dressed. They had a school of dancing from the loop . . . with some Irish name anyway. They were American style dancers not Irish dancers. They would put on some sketch of the jig.[2]

Roche's comments indicate that the promoters imitated what they saw drawing crowds at other concessions, and the dancers performing at the Village attempted an ersatz version of Irish dancing. The entertainment did not meet the approval of some members of the Catholic Church. When the Irish Village was forced to close for financial reasons, the Church attributed the Irish community's lack of support to "the demand for clean entertainment inspired by the Legion of Decency." An article appearing in the *New World* explained:

Disgusted by the cheap side shows which with their vulgarity and indecency disgraced the name and glory of Ireland, Irish men and women, together with other lovers of decency have withheld their patronage to such an extent that last week the Village was forced to close because of financial difficulties.[3]

The Legion of Decency was a group within the Catholic Church concerned with the effect popular entertainment was having on the morals of their members, particularly on the young. The Legion became best known for its movie rating system, that determined which movies were appropriate for which age group, which were "morally objectionable in part," and which were "condemned."

As reported in the *Chicago Tribune,* the Irish Village reopened "presenting a typically Irish program."[4] The Village was reorganized under the amended bankruptcy act and a trustee was appointed to oversee the operation. The reorganization and reopening of the Irish Village was publicized in the *New World* as being "A New Deal in the Irish Village," and

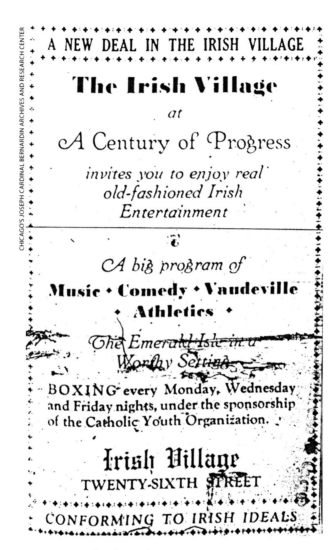

A NEW DEAL IN THE IRISH VILLAGE

The Irish Village

at

cA Century of Progress

invites you to enjoy real
old-fashioned Irish
Entertainment

cA big program of
Music • Comedy • Vaudeville
• Athletics •

The Emerald Isle in a
Worthy Setting

BOXING every Monday, Wednesday
and Friday nights, under the sponsorship
of the Catholic Youth Organization.

Irish Village
TWENTY-SIXTH STREET

CONFORMING TO IRISH IDEALS

23. Irish Village Advertisement, *New World*, 1934.

the display advertisement emphasized "real Irish entertainment . . . conforming to Irish ideals." [Fig. 23]

As a result of the reorganization, new, local Irish entertainers were enlisted: Mae Kennedy Kane, a former pupil of John McNamara, and Pat
Roche, a step dancer who had then been living in Chicago for about four

24. Pat Roche at the Irish Village, 1934.

years. [Figs. 24-25] Roche was asked to be master of ceremonies for the Irish entertainment. When asked why he was chosen for the job, Roche explained that they wanted authenticity, and since he was an entertainer of sorts, and from Ireland, they hired him.[5] In order to add to the au-

25. May Kennedy Kane at the Irish Village, 1934.

thenticity, Roche organized the Harp and Shamrock Orchestra, a group of Irish musicians who provided music for the Irish dancers. The group included Pat Richardson, a drummer from Tipperary; Joe Shannon, an uillean piper from Mayo; Eleanor Kane, a pianist from Chicago; Jim Devine, a fiddler from Limerick; and John Gaffney, an accordion player from Roscommon. [Fig. 26] Roche and the musicians achieved distinction by recording on the Decca label, on which Pat danced "The Blackbird" and "The Garden of Daisies" accompanied by the orchestra. The group was called an orchestra, rather than a ceili band. The term "ceili band" only developed during the 1950s; prior to that time, Irish musical groups were just referred to as Irish bands or orchestras.[6]

Also appearing at the Irish Village as part of the "new deal" were the O'Connor Family, the most famous member of which was the actor, singer, and dancer, Donald O'Connor. They did not perform any Irish

26. Harp and Shamrock Orchestra, 1934. Seated: Pat Richardson,
Joe Shannon, Pat Roche, Eleanor Kane Neary, Jim Devine,
John Gaffney. Standing: Peter Bolton, Violet Danaher.

dancing as part of the act, but Roche remembers teaching Donald a few hornpipe steps that summer.[7]

Along with the professional dancers, children from various Irish dancing schools were also invited to perform. By this time, Roche had been teaching dancing in Chicago for a couple of years, and so he was able to provide a group of students for regular appearances at the Irish Village. [Fig. 27] Likewise, Mae Kennedy Kane and her pupils performed on a regular basis. Jackie Hagerty and his dance partner, Dolores Kelly, were among Kennedy Kane's featured students. [Fig. 28] To encourage attendance at the Village, a dance competition was held that was won by Agnes Cavanaugh, one of Paul Dillon's pupils. Kate Bell Downs and Loretto Schaar Kistinger, two of Roche's dancers who appeared regularly at the Irish Village, fondly remember the experience. In order to enter the grounds without paying, they were issued official photo IDs. The fact that they performed at the Century of Progress distinguished them, and

27. Roche Dancers at Irish Village, 1934. Joe Cullinan,
Lillian Doolin, Florence Drennan, Eileen Pembroke,
Kate Bell, Loretto Schaar.

Downs remembers that her family proudly informed visiting relatives of this. Both took dance lessons from Roche at St. Gabriel's, a predominantly Irish parish on the south side. Downs observed that she and the other dancers were really just the "warm-up act" for Roche, since he was the one the audience really wanted to see. He always danced at the end of their performances and inevitably "he'd pull down the house."[8]

Kathleen Winkler and Loretta Mungovan, cousins who were accomplished step dancers, also regularly appeared at the Village. [Fig. 29] Roche recalled that they had taken lessons from the Lynch sisters, who were themselves former students of Professor McNamara.[9] Winkler and Mungovan had previously performed at Irish functions at which Pat Roche and the Shannon Rovers, a local pipe band, had also appeared. At one such event, a program at St. Mel's on the west side, the pastor was so impressed with the program that he asked Roche to start a dance class at the parish. Roche agreed, and subsequently that class developed into one of Roche's most popular classes.

28. Jackie Hagerty and Dolores Kelly at Irish Village, 1934.

According to Roche, the entertainment committee was constantly trying to come up with ways to get Chicagoans to visit to the Irish Village. As he commented, during the Depression money was tight and people were concerned with keeping a job and making a living.[10] One way they promoted the Village was by featuring boxing matches, part of the program then being sponsored by the Catholic Youth Organization (CYO). The previous year the Irish boxing team had visited the Century of Progress and had been involved in a match at Soldier Field. Boxing was regarded

29. Kathleen Winkler and Loretta Mungovan,
Irish Village, 1934.

as a wholesome pastime for youth, and the Irish community had a tradition of supporting this activity. Boxing therefore strengthened the image of decency that the village was trying to present, and which the Catholic Church would support. Another way the entertainment promoted attendance at the Irish Village was with a series of beauty contests that culminated in the crowning of a "Miss Shamrock," who would reign over Irish Day at the fair. That event was held on 15 August, on Our Lady Day in Harvest, a traditional feast day and celebration for the Irish. The *Chicago*

30. Program for *Pageant of the Celt,* 1934.

31. Actor appearing in *Pageant of the Celt.*

Tribune described the program as a "transplanted part of Ireland, and is replete with speeches, music, jigs, reels, and ballads."[11] The main address was broadcast over radio station WGN.

Pageant of the Celt

In addition to the Irish Village at the Century of Progress, another exceptional event also took place in the summer of 1934. *The Pageant of the Celt* was staged in Soldier Field on August 28 and 29. [Fig. 30] In early June, publicity on the event appeared in the *New World:* "The pageant will portray vividly, in action, song and story, the most prominent peaks in the story of Ireland and her people, her glorious and illustri-

32. Actors in *Pageant of the Celt.*

ous past, with a glance into her promising future."[12] The pageant's promoters stressed the authenticity of the project. For instance, one *New World* article explained that the Irish Costume Society of Dublin would assist in the costume design for the pageant, because "this group is the one body in the world able to speak with authority concerning the dress which the inhabitants of Ireland have worn throughout the ages."[13] [Figs. 31-33] The promoter of the pageant was John V. Ryan, a Chicago attorney. He recruited Edward J. Scanlon, stage director of the Munic-

33. Actors in *Pageant of the Celt.*

ipal Opera of St. Louis, as master director of the pageant. Local talent formed the thousand-member chorus and the five-hundred-member dance troupe. Michael MacLiammóir, from the Gate Theater in Dublin, happened to be in Chicago at the time and was chosen as the narrator. Dennis Cox, the Irish baritone who had been appearing at the Irish Village, was chosen as lead singer. Both Peter Bolton and Violet Danaher also appeared in the Pageant. Evidently, Mae Kennedy Kane, Paul Dillon, and Pat Roche all consulted with the producers on the dance portion of the program, although the dancing was not specifically mentioned in the articles other than to note that five hundred people would be involved in the dance.[14] Francis O'Neill was the chairman of the music committee. Two other local people also helped select and arrange the music: William Canole, an Irish musician who hosted an Irish radio program, and William Breen, a graduate of the Royal Irish Academy of Music in Dublin. Benedict Fitzgerald, the chief conductor of the pageant, was from Boston, but had made a "special study of Irish music during a long residence in Ireland."[15]

The pageant was publicized in the *Tribune* with articles and photos spanning the ten day period before it opened; and two days before the pageant, on August 26, a special program was aired over WGN radio featuring the principals of the cast. Michael MacLiammór recited scenes from several Irish plays, while Benedict Fitzgerald played some of his own arrangements of Celtic folk dances and also accompanied Dennis Cox. A review of the production appeared in the *Tribune* on 29 August, after the premiere but before the final performance. After describing the highlights of the pageant, the writer concluded: "So the story of Ireland was told last night, as it will be told again tonight in the same pageant. It is a story to which no Irishman's heart can fail to thrill."[16] Based on the reporter's comments, the producers succeeded in their goal.

Such highly publicized large-scale events as the Irish Village and the *Pageant of the Celt* helped to promote an awareness of Irish dancing and spotlighted Irish talent in the city. Nancy O'Malley Scoville, one of Pat Roche's pupils, explained that her father saw Roche dance at the World's Fair and, when she was old enough to start lessons, he searched out Roche and enrolled her in the class. Her father had been so impressed with his dancing that he wanted his daughter to take lessons specifically from Roche.[17]

The Shannon Rovers

Even though these larger but relatively short-lived events spotlighted Irish culture for the general public, it was the continued promotion of the music and dance within the Irish community itself that was the lifeblood of the dancing. The larger events helped establish the reputation of some of the performers, but the small-scale, consistent activities spon-

34. Shannon Rovers Pipe Band, World's Fair Irish Village, 1934.

sored by groups in the community were the key. Exhibitions of Irish dancing were typically featured at parties and events sponsored by Irish social clubs and groups. One organization in particular, the Shannon Rovers Irish Pipe Band, consistently sponsored events at which music and dancing were an integral component. [Fig. 34] The band and club had been organized in 1926 by Tommy Ryan, who emigrated from Limerick in 1923. [Fig. 35] Pat Roche began his performance career as the Drum Major for this band. During the 1930s and 1940s, Roche's dancers were typically part of the entertainment at events sponsored by the Shannon Rovers. For instance, in the summer of 1935, the club sponsored a boat trip on Lake Michigan which promised that "Pat Roche champion Irish step dancer with a group of amateurs will entertain."[18] For its St. Patrick's Day party in 1937, the club had a picture promoting the event on the front page of the *Garfieldian,* a neighborhood newspaper. The photograph featured Peggy Sheridan, one of Roche's dancers, and Daniel Russell, one of the pipers from the band. [Fig. 36] Each year the club sponsored a St. Patrick's Day dance which typically featured a performance by the pipe band, Irish and American dancing with separate bands

35. Tommy Ryan, Founder of Shannon Rovers Pipe Band.

for each type, and an exhibition by younger step dancers. By 1947, the club was advertising its fifteenth annual St. Patrick's dance and both Pat Roche's and Paul Dillon's dancers were on the program. To promote their St. Patrick's dance in 1952, the Shannon Rovers marched, along with the St. Mel High School Band, for about a mile down Madison Street, a main thoroughfare through the west side neighborhoods.[19]

36. Peggy Sheridan and Daniel Russell.

37. Mummers' Dance: Mary Ellen McCarthy, Mary Fitzpatrick,
Kathleen Nolan, Marilyn Martha, Marie Sullivan, Irene Wrenn,
Anna Marie Dillon, Norine Russell, Marian O'Brien, Eileen McNamara.

38. Shamrock American Club, St. Patrick's Day,1946. Pipers Phillip and Patrick
Boyle. Step dancers front: Mary Carroll, Kathleen Carroll, Peggy Shevlin;
back: Mary Heneghan, Mary Shevlin, Anne Heneghan, Nancy O'Malley.

IRISH
STEP AND FOLK DANCING
— TAUGHT BY AN EXPERT —

7111 S. RACINE AVE. (Hill Top Club)........MONDAY 7 P.M.
ST. MEL'S (Westside).........................SATURDAY 10 A. M.
4206 N. BROADWAY.............................FRIDAY 7 P. M.
2945 N. LUNA AVENUE.......................SATURDAY 1 P. M.

IRISH MUSIC TAUGHT
CHILDREN'S IRISH FLUTE BAND by Bob Flatley
4206 N. BROADWAY.............................FRIDAY 7 P. M.
1514 W. 73rd STREET.........................THURSDAY 7 P. M.

ROCHE'S SCHOOL
OF MUSIC AND DANCING
Often Imitated but never Duplicated
TELEPHONE DEARBORN 3776

39. Roche's School of Music and Dance Advertisement, 1937.

The Mummers' Club

Another group which was active during this era was the Mummers' Club. Paul Dillon was the dance teacher involved with this group, and his dancers were known for the "Mummers' Dance," in which they held sticks and used them as part of the dance. The tradition of mumming in Ireland is associated with the County Wexford, and a description printed in a pamphlet on Irish dance states:

> A set of Mummers is led by Captain who recites the Captain's rhyme and introduces his men. They perform two dances starting with the *claibh* and concluding with the reel. They dance in time with the music and strike perfect time with wooden sticks, or "swords" as they were often called.[20]

A 1937 article in the *Garfieldian* advertised a dance sponsored by the Mummers' Club and mentioned that "novelty dance numbers by Paul Dillon's dancing girl team" would be a feature. The next summer, the club staged a

"Night in Erin" in Garfield Park. The program included music and dancing and Paul Dillon was listed as the director of the show. An article promoting the event mentions that "Paul Dillon will direct the Irish Mummers in the Ritual dance," and mentioned that step dancing would be on the program as well.[21] The Mummers' Club also sponsored dances at other times. At the club's fall dance in 1938, Dillon's pupils performed and also sponsored a contest for the best Irish dancers. Also, as part of the publicity for various St. Patrick's Day celebrations in 1948, a picture of Paul Dillon's students posing for the Mummers' Dance appeared in the *Garfieldian*.[22] [Fig. 37] No mention of the Mummers' Club appears after the late 1940s.

The Ulster Liberty Legion and the Shamrock American Club also provided venues for Irish dancing performances. Several leaders of the former group had children who took dance lessons from Pat Roche; consequently, Roche's dancers provided the entertainment for club functions. Throughout the 1940s and into the 1950s the club held an annual St. Patrick's Day dance, as well as summer picnics or other events during the year. The Shamrock American Club also had many parents of Roche dancers among its membership. An article listing the St. Patrick's Day activities scheduled for 1946 mentions that "Pat Roche, the Irish dance master, and his team of Gaelic dancers" would be at the club's party and a picture of the dancers appeared in the *Lakeview Booster*, a north side neighborhood paper.[23] [Fig. 38]

Pat Roche and the Harp and Shamrock Club

The organization that seems to have been most consistently involved with Irish dancing was the Harp and Shamrock Club. It is also the group with which Roche was most intimately involved. The Harp and Shamrock title had been used for the orchestra Roche assembled for the Irish Village and, after the Century of Progress was over, the name was used for the club. A newspaper article appearing in 1938 explained: "The Harp and Shamrock club was organized three years ago for the purpose of keeping alive the music, dance and song of the Gael, and all funds derived from socials go to a fund for that purpose."[24]

The club sponsored numerous and varied events. In 1937 the Harp and Shamrock Club held an "Irish Festival," which included a movie of the All-Ireland finals in hurling and football, as well as entertainment by

40. Harp and Shamrock Flute Band, 1938. Top: Joe Cullinan,
Margaret Corrigan, Lucille McKillop, Veronica McGreal, Francis McGee,
Catherine Doyle, Mary Ellen Griffen, Frances Murphy, Florence Ferguson,
Mary Nagle, Raymond Murphy. Center: Bob Matthews, Tom Nagle,
Tom Murphy, Melvin Rose, Rita Reidy, Connie Brannigan, Pat Fergus.
Bottom: Margie Murphy (Drum Major), Bob Flatley (Instructor),
Mary Donnelly, Virginia Murray, James McInerney, Peggy Sheridan,
Jack Brown, Helen Cavanaugh, Michael Doyle,
Pat Roche (Manager), Annette Murphy (Drum Major).

Roche's dancers and band. During 1938, several articles and advertisements appeared in the *American Gael* promoting events sponsored by the
club and Roche's School of Music and Dancing. Pat Roche organized a
flute band for youngsters and expanded his dance classes to four different
locations around the city. [Fig. 39] Roche himself was not a musician, but
he thought that it was important to involve young people in Irish music
as well as dance, so he organized the band. He secured the assistance of
Bob Flatley, a flute player, to teach the students how to play the instru-

Harp and Shamrock
DANCING SCHOOL

In All Sections of the City
Under the Direction of Pat Roche

— DANCING CLASSES —

SOUTH SIDE
7109 S. Racine Ave.
Tuesday, 7-9 p. m.

WEST SIDE
4319 Washington Blvd.
Saturday, 10-11:30 a. m.

NORTH SIDE
4206 Broadway
Friday, 7-9 p. m.

NORTHWEST
1352 N. Monitor Ave.
Saturday, 12:30-2 p. m.

NORTHWEST
2945 N. Luna Ave.
Saturday, 2:30-4 p. m.

— MUSIC CLASSES —

SOUTH SIDE
1514 W. 73rd St.
Thursday, 7-9 p. m.

NORTH SIDE
4206 Broadway
Friday, 7-9 p. m.

— DRUMMING CLASSES —

WEST SIDE
4721 Madison St

41. Harp and Shamrock Dancing School Advertisement, 1938.

ments. Irish music and dance certainly complement each other and the promotion of one positively affects the promotion of the other. Many of Roche's dancers were also members of the band or had siblings who were members. The dancers and the flute band performed at the functions sponsored by the club. In fact, one of the dances sponsored by the club in 1938 was for the benefit of the children's Irish flute band. [Fig. 40]

Roche had great plans for the flute band which he hoped to take to the 1939 World's Fair to be held in New York City. During 1938, several display advertisements and articles appeared in the *American Gael* encouraging parents to enroll their children in the band in order to be part of the trip to New York. The Harp and Shamrock Club even hosted a card party to raise money to buy more flutes for the band. Although the trip never

42. Murphy Sisters with Pat Roche.

materialized, the band did stay in existence. By 1940, the band and the dancers were advertised under the title of the Harp and Shamrock. Dance classes were being offered in five different locations around the city, music lessons in two locations, and a special drumming class in yet another locale. [Fig. 41] Ultimately, Roche turned the band over completely to Flatley. The group then became known as the Star of Freedom Flute Band and continued to perform at social functions across the city.

Even though the band was Irish, baton twirlers accompanied the group. [Fig. 42] They must have added a particularly American flavor, since baton twirling is not exactly an activity indigenous to Ireland. However, baton twirling was popular at the time in Chicago, and it found its way not only into the flute band, but also into the Irish dance numbers. Roche developed a novelty routine in which the Murphy sisters, Annette and Marjorie, who were accomplished baton twirlers, would dance the jig while twirling the baton. In several articles and advertisements which appeared in 1938, the Murphys are listed as one of the features in Roche's entertainment package. Lucille and Rosalina McKillop, two of Roche's dancers from that era, remembered the Murphy sisters, but explained that they, too, performed the same novelty number. Roche recalled that, spurred on by the feats of the Murphys and McKillops, several other dancers came up with novelty numbers.[25] For instance, Peggy Sheridan worked a yo-yo while dancing the hornpipe. Mary Ann Carr danced the hornpipe on a table upon which plates were placed at each corner, completing the dance without any of the plates falling off.[26] As improbable as this may sound, John Cullinane cites other precedents for this type of exhibition:

> in the last century and start of this century bouts of solo dancing were most frequently performed on the top of the table, or barrel or even on the top of the half door and the dancing was frequently in either the kitchen or tap room in a bar. . . . In fact in those days it was the greatest tribute that could be payed to a dancer to say that they could dance on the top of a plate, even smaller than the barrel top . . . . The implication was that the smaller the space the neater and nicer the performance.[27]

Granted, Roche's dancer did not dance on the plate, but she did dance on the table top and had a plate in close proximity. The main point of the display was to show the neatness and precision of the dancer.

The Harp and Shamrock Club also sponsored various trips and excursions that included Irish entertainment as part of the package. Boat cruises on Lake Michigan and excursions to smaller lakes outside the city were advertised. Trips of a religious nature were also offered. Annual pilgrimages to Holy Hill, located in southern Wisconsin, were quite popular. The area had been settled by Irish who emigrated after the famine in 1847. As described in an *American Gael* article in 1939: "Holy Hill is the Lourdes of America where many benefits have been received."[28] As part of the outing, entertainment was provided both on the bus trip and at the location itself after the devotional activities concluded. Roche also tried to organize a trip to Irish Day at the World's Fair in New York City during the summer of 1939. At times it is difficult to distinguish which activities were promoted solely by Roche and which were under the auspices of the Harp and Shamrock Club, since the two had become somewhat synonymous.

Commercial, Parish, and Community Sponsors
In addition to opportunities provided by the various social clubs, commercial establishments also provided venues for dancing. Following the Century of Progress, several events were held which featured various performers from the Irish Village. In April 1935, Peter Bolton, cited as "World's Champion Irish Step Dancer," and Pat Roche, advertised as "American Champion Irish Step Dancer," appeared together at The Viking Temple Ballroom on the north side. Appearing along with "Pete and Pat," were seventy dance students. [Fig. 43] In October of the same year, a display advertisement announced that "Irish Night" would be sponsored by the Blue Goose, a restaurant on the west side of the city. Pat Roche was one of the featured entertainers along with Agnes Cavanaugh, the dancer who had won the dance contest held at the Irish Village at the Century of Progress. [Fig. 44] Other establishments also received publicity for the Irish entertainment they provided on the premises. Just one example is Gannon's Hall at 7109 S. Racine. Movie distributors also provided an Irish stage show to accompany films about Ireland. In December of 1938, the film, *Dawn Over Ireland,* was shown at several locations and Roche's dancers were part of the evening's performance. [Fig. 45] Another Irish film, *Kathleen,* was advertised a couple of years later and Irish music and dance were featured along with that movie.

Roman Catholic parishes and schools that had large Irish populations also sponsored events at which Irish dancing was performed. Paul Dillon provided the entertainment for the St. Ignatius Mothers' Club at one of its meetings in 1935.[29] His niece remembers that Dillon was also regularly involved with the annual St. Patrick's Day program which was produced at Presentation parish on the west side, where he conducted dance lessons.[30]

Similarly, Pat Roche and his dancers were part of the St. Patrick's Day program held each year at St. Gabriel's Parish. Roche resided in St. Gabriel's when he first arrived in Chicago, started his first dance class in that parish, and continued teaching there for many years. Kate Bell

Appearing Here - Appearing Here

SEE PETE and PAT

Dancing Side by Side

 Peter Bolton

World's Champion
Irish Step Dancer

Pat Roche

American Champion
Irish Step Dancer

WITH A CAST OF 70 STUDENTS DANCING THE TRADITIONAL STANDARIZED STEP AND
FOLK DANCES OF IRELAND, LASTING ONE AND HALF HOURS.

At the

Viking Temple Ballroom

3255 North Sheffield Avenue

Friday Evening, April 26th, 1935

Curtain roll at 8 o'clock   Admission 35 Cents

To be Followed by Irish and American Dancing Until ?
Music by Roche's Harp and Shamrock Orchestra

185 Schornwald Print 2853 Archer Ave.

43. "Pat and Pete" Advertisement, 1935.

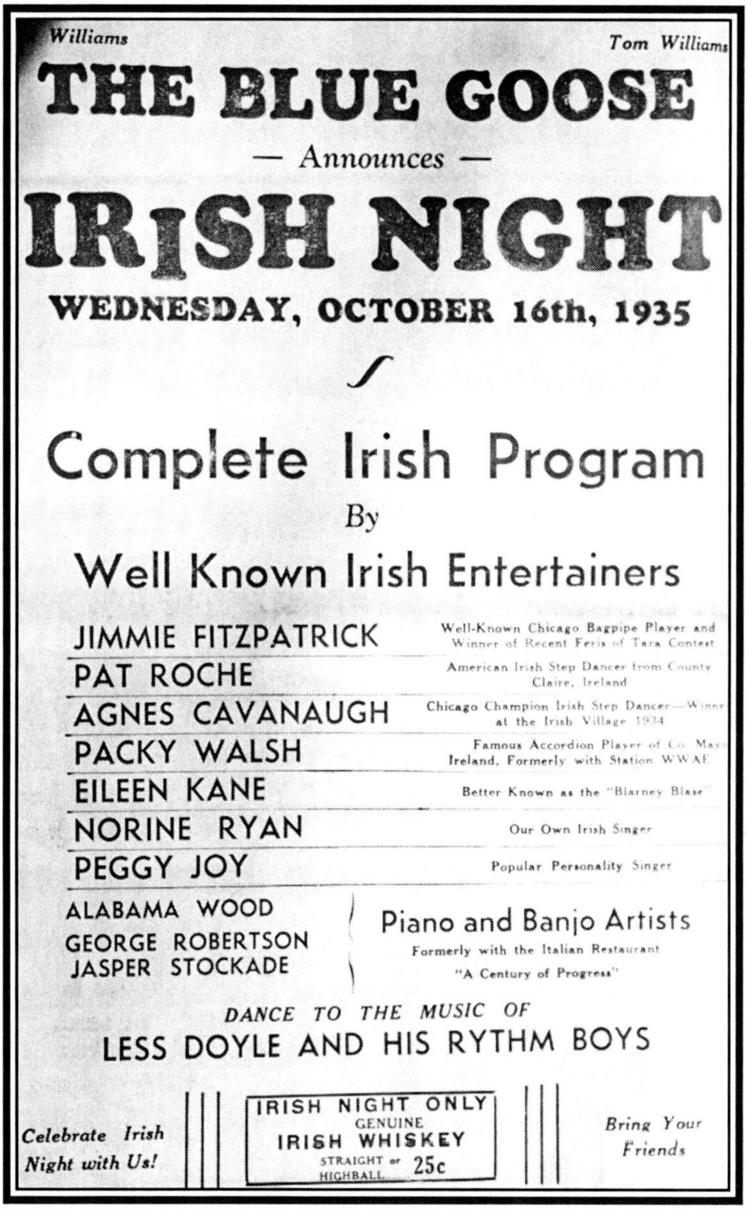

44. Blue Goose Advertisement.

AMERICAN GAEL DECEMBER 1938. COURTESY THE ROCHE FAMILY

Three Nights in Ireland

FIRST NORTH SIDE SHOWING!!

DIRECT FROM DUBLIN

"DAWN OVER IRELAND"

ACTUAL I. R. A. VETS IN ACTION

HEAR THE I. R. A. CALLED TO ARMS!
SEE THE BLACK AND TANS AMBUSHED!
— FEEL THE PULSE OF IRELAND!

First Authentic Film of the 'Trouble'

In Addition

Huge Irish Stage Show

PAT ROCHE'S DANCING SCHOOL

BILLY RALEIGH — CHICAGO'S "BOBBY BREEN"
THE HARP AND SHAMROCK CLUB
THE IRISH FLUTE BAND
THE MURPHY SISTERS

THURSDAY, DECEMBER 15

MIDWAY CASINO   2650 Lincoln Ave.

FRIDAY, DECEMBER 16

QUEEN OF ANGELS AUDITORIUM   4530 N. Western

SATURDAY, DECEMBER 17

ST. HENRY'S PARISH HALL   1920 Devon Ave.

ADMISSION FIFTY CENTS
CHILDREN 15c   SHOW STARTS AT 8:15 & 10:30

45. *Dawn Over Ireland* advertisement.

Downs, who was one of Roche's first pupils at St. Gabriel's, remembers the popularity of those parish programs. The productions were so popular that they would run for a whole week in order to accommodate all who wanted to attend. She and Loretto Schaar Kistinger, another one of Roche's pupils from that time, agreed that the highlight of their dancing experience was being asked by Roche to dance with him during the finale of the show.[31] Traditionally, Roche would dance alone at the end of the program, but on one occasion he asked them to join him in the closing number. Another example of a church-sponsored event was advertised in the *Garfieldian* in March of 1950. Our Lady of Sorrows Parish sponsored a dance and variety show and anticipated that it would draw about 2,000 people. The article mentions that Roche would demonstrate Irish dances.[32]

On occasion, benefit parties were held for members of the Irish community who were experiencing financial distress, and these functions also provided an opportunity for the Irish dancers to perform. For instance, a 1940 article mentions that dancers from the Lynch sisters' school were performing at a benefit, along with a group of children from the Harp and Shamrock school.[33] The Lynch sisters, Mary and Lucille, taught dancing on the south side of the city, and were former pupils of Professor McNamara.

Exhibitions of Irish dancing were sponsored in Chicago by Irish social clubs as part of their numerous and varied activities, at commercial establishments, at Catholic schools and parishes, and by those conducting charitable events for the benefit of someone in the community. During the 1930s and 1940s, large festivals were jointly sponsored by various individuals and organizations. Typically, these celebrations would take place during the summer, most often near the date of 15 August, the traditional Our Lady Day in Harvest in Ireland. In 1937, such an event was publicized in the *Garfieldian*. A Gaelic Festival was to feature "athletic games, juvenile Irish step dancing and senior events; songs by radio stars; state title event for girls' softball throw; races; Scottish dancers; war pipers in ancient Gaelic melodies; and an exhibition by Mary Kelly All-Ireland dancing champion."[34] Jackie Hagerty, who had appeared at the Irish Village as one of Mae Kennedy Kane's pupils, had started his own dancing school, and his class was among the dance groups involved with the Gaelic

46. Jackie Hagerty and Students Kathryn Ready
and Mary Therese Keating, c. 1940.

Festival. [Fig. 46] The event was postponed for a week because of the wet
grounds at Mill Stadium where it was scheduled to be held:

> All talent will remain here to participate including Mary Kelly of
> Ireland; Walter Curran, Irish tenor; Billy Raleigh, Irish tenor; Smil-
> ing Bill Mahoney, Jackie Hagerty and his Irish dancers and Mae
> Kennedy Kane. The Irish Mummers club, represented by Paul Dil-
> lon and a group of dancers, will be present.[35]

Today, it is nearly impossible to postpone an event, because performers
usually have other commitments and facilities are booked for other en-
gagements.

In August 1938, the second annual Irish Day celebration was held at Riverview Park. Publicity for the event appeared in both the *Garfieldian* and the *American Gael*. Dance contests were held, but no formal program or list of events was printed. The dance contests represented only a small part of the day's activities; athletic events, a beauty contest, and a contest to see which county in Ireland was most represented at the celebration were also features of the day. Irish Day, or Lady Day in Harvest as it was often called, continued for many years. In later years, the event was organized primarily by Mae Kennedy Kane. A 1945 *Garfieldian* article included a list of teachers whose dancers would be performing: Mae Kennedy Kane, Mary and Lucille Lynch, Paul Dillon, Madonna Gaffney (substituting for Jackie Hagerty who was in the armed services), Rose Ann Smith, Theresa Prendergast, Marge Corrigan, and Mary Terese O'Malley.[36] Marge Corrigan was a former student of Pat Roche's, and Rose Ann Smith and Theresa Prendergast were previously Paul Dillon's students.

First Chicago Feis, 1945

The most significant event in the development of Irish dancing in Chicago was the commencement of the Irish National Feis in 1945 by Pat Roche and the Harp and Shamrock Club. Several factors distinguished this feis. Contestants from across the United States would participate—the feis was national in scope. Prior to the organization of the feis in Chicago, Roche had been taking his dancers out of town to compete and perform. In the early 1940s he took his dancers to New York for the annual feis held at Fordham University. In New York at that time, Professor James McKenna, a native of County Kerry, was the primary dance teacher and was very involved with the promotion of Irish dancing. In fact, when Roche first came over from Ireland in 1925, he lived for several years in New York before heading west to Chicago. During the late 1920s, he himself took dance lessons from McKenna. In those days, McKenna's dancers were considered the teams to beat in competition.

It was very significant that the team Roche took to New York defeated the McKenna dancers. Lucille and Rosalina McKillop, who were members of that winning team, stated that although the victory was exciting for them as dancers, it was only as adults that they fully appreciated the true significance that victory had for Roche.[37] They had defeated dancers

47. Roche's Dancers at the 1946 Feis. Front: Joan Smith, Noreen Gibbons, Nancy Cunningham, Kay Cloughessy, and Joann Brow. Back: Peggy Mulvihill, Pat Roche (teacher), Eileen Ring, Joe Cullinan.

trained by McKenna, the teacher from whom Roche had taken lessons and whom Roche greatly admired. In addition to the feis, Roche's dancers also participated in National Folk Festivals in Philadelphia and Washington, D.C. The McKillops suggested that the interest in folk festivals in the early 1940s was in part an attempt to bring nationalities together in order to help unify the country's war effort. After watching the Lithuanian dancers perform at one of these festivals, they incorporated a few of the

Lithuanian dance movements into their own three-hand reel. As a result of their appearances around the country, Roche and his dancers became known outside the Chicago area.

The feis organizers in New York encouraged Roche to start a feis in Chicago and promised to advise him and send competitors to support the endeavor. On Wednesday, 15 August 1945, Chicago's First Annual Irish Feis was sponsored by the Harp and Shamrock Club at Pilsen Park at 26th and Albany Streets. A copy of the promotional letter sent by the organizers mentions that the series of competitions was arranged principally for the younger generation. This emphasis differs from that of the two feiseanna that had been sponsored by the Gaelic League in Chicago in 1912 and 1913. Those events catered to adult contestants as well as young people. In Ireland there was also a shift in the age group participating in competitions. At the turn of the century, dancers who competed in Ireland were typically aged fourteen to forty, but by the 1930s, six- to eighteen-year-olds had come to dominate the competitions.[38] A month before the Chicago feis, an article announcing it appeared in the *Garfieldian,* with another article appearing each week before the event. Reportedly, contestants from New York, Boston, and Philadelphia were registered for the competitions. It was announced that one of the trophies was named after John E. McNamara, the great Chicago dance teacher.

The second distinguishing feature of the Harp and Shamrock Feis was its continuity. The event started in 1945 and was held consecutively for seventeen years, after which time sponsorship of the Chicago feis was taken over by a different organization. During the Harp and Shamrock years, the feis changed locations and dates, but the event continued to be held every summer and continued to attract dancers from around the country.

The Chicago Feis, 1946-1952
In 1946, an article promoting the second annual feis stated that 750 contestants would be competing in 84 different events. [Fig. 47] Entries were from New York, Cleveland, St. Louis, Philadelphia, Detroit, and Peoria.[39] [Figs. 48] A picture of both Roche and McKenna appeared in the *Garfieldian* along with the explanation that they were coaches of competing dance teams. [Fig. 49] The friendly rivalry between the two dancing schools continued. In June of 1947, Roche took his dancers to the New

IRELAND'S NATIONAL
FEIS

● NEW YORK ● BOSTON ● PHILADELPHIA
● DETROIT ● CLEVELAND and ● CHICAGO

COMPETING FOR NATIONAL HONORS IN

EIGHTY-SIX COMPETITIVE EVENTS

Presenting

THE GREATEST ARRAY OF IRISH TALENT

In Music, Dance, Song, Oratory, Gaelic Speaking, Etc. in the Nation

At Spacious **PILSEN PARK**, 26th and Albany Ave.

on

Thursday, August 15th, 1946

Continuing from Noon to Midnight
Under the Auspices of

THE HARP AND SHAMROCK CLUB of CHICAGO

——Supported by Twelve Other Irish American Croops——

457

(OVER)

SPECIAL COMPETITION #87

Award—Dean Clark Trophy

Open to all teachers, professionals and former 1st prize senior medal winners of the New York or Chicago Feis.

Competitors must dance the Jig, Hornpipe and one of the following set pieces:

     a. The Blackbird
     b. The Job Of Journeywork
     c. The Garden of Daisies

ENTRY BLANK

Competitors Name..

Address..

Competition No...

Mail Entry Blanks to HARP AND SHAMROCK CLUB
3240 W. Harrison St., Chicago 24, Illinois

87 Separate Competitions — Write in for Syllabus

(OVER)

48. 1946 Feis Postcard and Entry Form.

49. James McKenna and Pat Roche.

50. Winners at the 1947 New York Feis. Top: Frank Culhane, Helen Griffin, Mary Donelan, Catherine Dalton, Jim Shea, Peggy Mulvihill, Eileen Ring, Jack Moriarty. Center: Bernadine Fallon, Nancy O'Malley, Mary Campbell, Mary Lou Corbett, Rosemary O'Malley, Mary Heneghan, Mary Shevlin. Bottom: Pat Roche, Tommy Hallissey, unknown, Rosemary Boyle, Anne Heneghan, Peggy Shevlin, Jimmy Daly, Joe Cullinan.

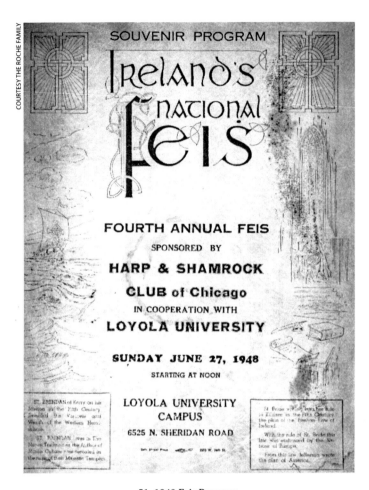

SOUVENIR PROGRAM

Ireland's
national
Feis

FOURTH ANNUAL FEIS

SPONSORED BY

HARP & SHAMROCK

CLUB of Chicago

IN COOPERATION WITH

LOYOLA UNIVERSITY

SUNDAY JUNE 27, 1948

STARTING AT NOON

LOYOLA UNIVERSITY
CAMPUS

6525 N. SHERIDAN ROAD

51. 1948 Feis Program.

York Feis and scored several victories over McKenna's dancers. [Fig. 50] Photographs of the victors appeared in both the *Daily News* and the *Sun-Times,* daily newspapers in Chicago. These photographs also helped publicize the Third Annual Chicago Feis scheduled for Pilsen Park on the Fourth of July, a switch from the usual 15 August date.

Even though Roche's and McKenna's dancers competed with each other, they shared steps and techniques. Both Nancy O'Malley Scoville and the McKillop sisters (who went to New York at different times) men-

52. Stages at 1948 Feis.

53. Stages at 1948 Feis.

tioned that their stay included a visit to McKenna's dance class and a step-swapping session with his dancers. Similarly, Roche recalled an occasion when McKenna and his dancers were in Chicago and they had a party for him at a fellow Kerryman's home. Both Roche and Dillon brought some of their dancers to the party, and during the evening McKenna's dancers shared their knowledge with them.

Again in 1948, the date of the feis changed, as well as the location. The Fourth Annual Chicago Feis was held on 27 June on the campus of Loyola University. The expanded space allowed Gaelic athletic games to be included in the day's activities. The program lists events in solo singing in Gaelic and English, choral groups, solo instrumental music, band competitions, recitations in Gaelic and English, Celtic design, and both solo and team dancing. [Fig. 51] Two events in solo Scottish dancing were also listed. Besides the usual dance competitions divided according to age groups, there was a championship competition for senior dancers over fourteen years old. [Figs. 52-53] Just as in 1946, there was also a special competition for teachers, professionals, or those who had previously won first place in the senior championship. There was a John E. McNamara trophy for the former competition and a Dean Clark trophy for the latter. These events had to be won twice in order for competitors to be able to keep the trophy permanently.

In 1949 the feis was again held at Loyola, but on 19 June. The program of events was about the same as the previous year, except that the senior championship trophy was now named in honor of Peter Bolton, the dancer from Ireland who had appeared at the Irish Village during the Century of Progress, and the other major trophy was named in honor of Rev. Lawrence Barry. The winners from the previous year had retired the other two trophies. The feis program for 1949 included the list of adjudicators. People who had either been dancers themselves or were knowledgeable about dancing were enlisted to judge the competitions. Margaret Hayes, Hannah Dalton, and Bernice Mahoney, all former students of Professor McNamara, appeared on the list of adjudicators. Roche met with the judges and explained the procedure to them before the competitions began. He developed the guidelines by consulting with adjudicators and teachers from other cities, and by asking for advice from dancers and teachers from Ireland. Roche commented that he had initially received

COURTESY NANCY O'MALLEY SCOVILLE

54. Nancy O'Malley and the
Ardagh Challenge Trophy, 1949.

instruction on judging techniques from Dennis Cox, the singer who had
been in Chicago for the Century of Progress and had done some judging
for dance competitions in Ireland before his visit to the United States.[40]
Ettie McPherson, who taught Scottish dancing in Chicago, explained the
guidelines used in judging Scottish dancing and Roche adapted some of
these to the Irish dance competitions.[41] The instructions and guidelines
distributed to the adjudicators asked them to consider four factors when
determining the final number of points allotted to each dancer: 1.) time
or rhythm, 2.) carriage or cooperation, 3.) execution or effect, and 4.) steps
or figure. Each contestant or team of dancers started with 100 points, with
deductions being made in each category as part of judging.

In order to encourage broader interest and participation in the 1949
feis, new promotional ideas were considered. A queen contest was a stan-

55. Pat Roche's 1947 Winning 8-Hand Reel. Back:
Joe Cullinan, Jack Moriarity, Jim Shea, Frank Culhane.
Front: Eileen Ring, Mary Shevlin, Mary Heneghan, Mary Campbell.

56. Jim Shea's Four-Hand Reel, 1948: M. McCarthy,
R. McGlynn, M. Laird, and M. Shea.

dard event, not only at the feis, but at almost every social gathering. On a different level, an essay contest for high school students was initiated by the feis committee to interest high school students in the proceedings. A replica of the Ardagh Chalice was ordered from Ireland and awarded to the high school attended by the contest's winner. The trophy stayed in the high school for the year, and only after the school had won it more than once would the trophy be retired to that school. Nancy O'Malley Scoville, who was also one of Roche's prize dancers, won the trophy for Immaculata High School. [Fig. 54] When the school was closing, the administrators called her to see if she would be interested in having the trophy. She immediately went to retrieve it, so this artifact has been preserved. Even though essay contests and other events were incorporated into the feis, the dancing remained the chief focus, and the dance competitions generated the most interest and participation.

In August 1949, Roche was once again involved with a celebration of Lady Day in Harvest. The *Garfieldian* explained that there would be a special contest for Chicago's best Irish step dancers. Dancers who had won titles at the National Feis held at Loyola earlier in the summer would compete again at this event for medals from Ireland. Pat Roche was cited as the entertainment chairman for the event.[42]

In 1948 and 1949, several dancers from the Roche's triumphant 1947 teams started their own dancing schools. Mary Shevlin McNamara, Mary Campbell Fahey, Jim Shea, Joe Cullinan, Eileen Ring, and Frank Culhane eventually started teaching. [Figs. 55-57] Even though some of Roche's pupils followed these dancers into their respective schools, the Harp and Shamrock dancers maintained a national reputation by traveling to competitions and events in other cities. [Figs. 58-59] The new teachers developed sizeable schools, but they concentrated more on local venues for their dancers. Their students participated in the annual Harp and Shamrock Feis, smaller competitions held in conjunction with Lady Day in Harvest celebrations, and all the usual social events sponsored by Irish social clubs and other organizations. Several of Mary Shevlin McNamara's students were among those pictured in the newspaper in August 1950 as they participated in "Tostal," a small-scale dance competition.[43] Mary Campbell Fahey, Jim Shea, and Frank Culhane all had dancers competing in the 1951 Harp and Shamrock Feis.

57. Mary Shevlin McNamara's Dancers, 1950s. Front: Ellen Shevlin, Joey White, Maureen Doyle, Jerry Rafferty. Back: Gene O'Sullivan, Susan Boyle, Jack O'Sullivan, Peggy Finnegan.

From 1948 through 1951, the feis was held at Loyola University, but in 1952 the site changed to St. Philip's High School Stadium. [Figs. 60-61] Richard J. Daley, then Cook County Clerk, was listed as Chairman of the event, with Roche as Program Director. Owing to the muddy condition of the field, the feis had to be postponed for a week. An article in the *Garfieldian* on 25 June 1952 stated:

County Clerk Richard J. Daley, chairman, announced that all the star talent has elected to stay here and compete Sunday. In addition, he said, many of the all-star dancers from New York who were unable to make the trip for last Sunday's feis will be on hand next Sunday.[44]

This paralleled the postponements of the Gaelic Festival in 1937 and the

58. Pat Roche Dancers, 1950s: Kathy Roche, Jeanne Howlett, Marie Walsh, Coletta Burke, Mary Ellen Halpin, unknown, unknown, Maureen Travers.

1950 feis held at Loyola. Roche recalled that on one of his trips to New York, the feis there got rained out, too. The organizers of that feis held a small competition in an indoor site in order to give the dancers who had traveled from other parts of the country a chance to compete. Clearly, postponing such huge events required impressive organization. According to Roche, these events were always a financial risk because bad weather could either diminish attendance or force postponement or cancellation. On more than one occasion, the organizers lost money on the events because of bad weather. In those instances, they were forced to hold dances or other events in order to cover the deficit. However, the risks involved did not deter the organizers from continuing to sponsor events for the Irish community. The Harp and Shamrock Feis continued to be held at Pilsen Park throughout the 1950s. [Fig. 62] Roche's teams continued to be contenders and were victorious on numerous occasions. [Fig. 63]

59. Pat Roche Dancers, 1950s: Back: Denise Geany,
Kathy Roche, Mary Ann Ryan. Front: unknown
and Roderick O'Connor.

By 1953, there were close to a dozen schools of Irish dancing in Chicago, spanning the city. There was an annual national feis that attracted Irish dancers from around the country; there were smaller, local dance contests; and there were numerous venues for dancing exhibitions provided by social clubs, commercial establishments, and Catholic schools and parishes. Irish dance had become a firmly established activity in the Irish-American community of Chicago.

Remembering Pat Roche
Pat Roche had a tremendous impact on Irish dance in Chicago during the 1930s, 40s, and 50s. Not only was he a great dancer, performer, and teacher, but he was also an organizer and promoter. Even as a youth back

8TH ANNUAL IRISH FEIS

ST. PHILIP'S STADIUM

3140 W. Van Buren St. at Kedzie Ave.

SUN., JUNE 22, 1952

COMMENCING AT 11:00 A. M.

SPONSORED BY THE

HARP & SHAMROCK CLUB, Inc.

1948 - 49		IRISH FEIS
CHICAGO		Held At
National Champion		Fordham University
IRISH DANCERS		N. Y. City
PUPILS OF PROF. PAT ROCHE		

65 - COMPETITIVE EVENTS - 65

New York - Detroit - St. Louis - Cleveland

CONTESTS

Irish Dancing - Scottish Dancing

MUSIC - SINGING - POETRY - STORY TELLING - BANDS

CELTIC ART EXHIBIT

ADMISSION $1.50 Tax Incl. "L" Trains Direct to Gate

60. 1952 Feis Poster.

61. Competitors at the 1952 Feis. Foreground: Mary Campbell's students,
Dennis Dennehy and Theresa Bennett.

in his village of Doonaha, County Clare, he organized the local football
team and negotiated with neighbors for a place to practice. On his boat
trip over to New York, he was instrumental in staging a tug-of-war between the crew of the ship and the Irish passengers on board. When he arrived in Chicago, after spending a few years in New York, he displayed
his entrepreneurial spirit by starting his own egg, tea, and coffee business,
which he eventually had to give up because of his involvement with the
Irish Village. During most of his life he worked two jobs, in addition to
teaching dancing several times a week and raising a family of eight children. He was a man of incredible energy and enthusiasm. Roche valued
the talents and expertise of others and was always willing to ask for their
assistance in order to complete certain projects. He had a genuine love of
Irish dance and music and always wanted to share this appreciation with
others. In Pat's own words, "I was always promoting something."[45] He died
in October 2004, just five months short of his 100th birthday. Irish dance
in Chicago owes him thanks for the work he did over the decades through
his promotion of the dance, music, and culture of Ireland.

62. 1954 Feis Poster.

63. Pat Roche Dancers. Back: Paddy Gilhooley, Jim Wallace, Sam McGarel, un-known. Front: Lu Hynes, Margie Bartishell, Marge Crotty, Kitty Gehrman.

CHAPTER 4

New Steps:
Expanding the Boundaries,
1953-1989

As dancing continued to become more popular, teachers more numerous, and dancing competitions both more regional and more national in character, the need to formulate guidelines became apparent. In the late 1940s and early 1950s there were attempts by dancing teachers in the United States to create an official organization. Pat Roche was involved with these efforts, and, in fact, was the first president of the Irish Dancing Teachers Commission of America (IDTCA), formed in 1953. Some of the first members of this group were Peggy and Peter Smith of New Jersey, Peter and Cyril McNiff of New York, Sean Lavery of Philadelphia, Josephine Moran of Massachusetts, and Professor James McKenna and Vincent O'Connor of New York.[1]

Irish Dancing Teachers Commission of America (IDTCA)
The IDTCA strived for national representation in its membership. In an advertisement for the IDTCA that appeared in the program for the Harp and Shamrock Club's 11th Annual National Feis (August 1955), the national officers were listed as: President, Pat Roche; Vice President, Sean Lavery; Treasurer, Helena Lynch; Secretary, Mary Margaret Shea; and, Sergeant-at-Arms, Donald MacDonald. The various state organizers were listed as: Michael J. (Joe) Cullinan, Chicago; Donald MacDonald, New York; John McErlean, Newark; George McLoughlin, Philadelphia; Eddie Masterson, Los Angeles; Josephine Moran, Cambridge, Massachusetts; and Daniel O'Connell, Dearborn, Michigan. [Fig. 64] Thus members were from both coasts and the Midwest, fulfilling the challenge to be national in character. There was significant participation on the local level as well. The Chicago Chapter members of the organization included: Mary Camp-

The Harp and Shamrock Club, Inc. of Chicago

11th Annual IRISH nacional feis

SOUVENIR
PROGRAM

IRISH YOUTH DAY

SATURDAY, AUGUST 20, 1955
At PILSEN PARK

64. 1955 Feis Program.

bell, Marge Corrigan, Frank Culhane, Michael (Joe) Cullinan, Margaret Hayes, Pat Roche, Jim Shea, and Mary Margaret Shea. A photograph taken in November 1955 shows members of the Chicago delegation to the IDTCA convention held in New York City. The group included Pat and Grace Roche, Mary Campbell, Mary Margaret Shea, Mary McNamara, Margaret Hayes, and a young Dennis Dennehy. [Fig. 65]

65. Chicago Delegation to the 1955 IDTCA Convention, New York City:
Pat Roche, Grace Roche, Mary Campbell, Mary Margaret Shea, Dennis Dennehy,
Margaret McNamara, Margaret Hayes.

The nascent organization faced many challenges. One of the biggest
problems was the tempo of the music being played for dancers. In the
1950s, feiseanna around the country all had their own rules and regulations
governing the competitions, and discrepancies arose with the lack of consistent guidelines. The old Cork/Kerry style of dancing that had been
prevalent in the United States during the first half of the century was being
challenged by a new, slower style of dancing developed in Northern Ireland, in Belfast and Derry, and introduced to the United States by new immigrants arriving in New York and Canada during the 1950s.[2] At feiseanna,
dancers were allowed to set their own tempo and to ask the musicians to
slow down or speed up the music before they began to dance. Dennis Dennehy commented that, in those days, how good a dancer was at judging
the tempo of the music made a significant difference in that dancer's success in competition.[3] In 1959, a group of teachers meeting in New York
devised a solution for the problem. Two tempos would be played for each
competition, slow and fast. The different times would be monitored by a
metronome so the tempo of the music would be consistent.[4]

66. Little Gaelic Singers, 1956.

The IDTCA began standardizing rules and regulations and establishing consistent guidelines for judging feiseanna. Roche commented that during these early years he had attempted to create more official ties to Ireland, but that the Irish Dancing Commission (An Coimisiún le Rincí Gaelacha) in Ireland did not seem interested in any collaboration with the U.S. organization. The IDTCA existed for several years, but was unable to survive into the next decade.

The New Style
A new era, beginning in the late 1950s, not only saw Irish dance beginning to become more structured and codified, but it also saw a change in the style of dancing. In addition to a slower tempo, this new style also incorporated more syncopated, aerial, diagonal, and circular movements. Chicago was not immune to these new trends, and various influences began to affect the style of dance in the city.

One of these influences was the Chicago appearance of "The Little Gaelic Singers," who hailed from County Derry. They appeared on the *Ed Sullivan Show* in October 1956, and in November they performed at Chicago's Orchestra Hall. [Fig. 66] The group of young performers sang, played musical instruments, and danced. The dancing was under the direction of Brendan De Glin, noted Derry dance teacher, adjudicator, and performer. Included in the first tour group was Ron Plummer, who ultimately emigrated to North America and became a certified teacher and adjudicator.

Witnessing the dance style of this group alerted Chicago dancers to the stylistic changes that were occurring. "The Little Gaelic Singers" came to Chicago on two more occasions. In May 1958, under the sponsorship of the Harp and Shamrock Club, they had two performances: the first was at Steinmetz High School, and the second at Calumet High School. In February 1959, they returned to Orchestra Hall for a Columban Sisters Benefit. Chicago dancers were quick to note the changes in style demonstrated by the Derry performers.

There were compelling influences affecting the style of dance, not only in performance, but also in competition. When the McNiff Dancers from New York and the dancers from the Butler Academy in Toronto started to compete at the Chicago Feis, the differences between the two styles, old and new, became very apparent. Teachers and dancers in Chicago wanted to be part of this new style.

Marge Bartishell, a former Roche student, became the catalyst for the development of the new style of dance in Chicago. Marge's partnership with her husband Dennis Dennehy, who had taken dancing from Mary Campbell Fahey, greatly influenced Irish dance in Chicago and guided it through the transition into a new era, an era that was structured and shaped by new national and international affiliations. In 1957, Marge began teaching in her mother's basement on Lowe Avenue, taking over Joe Cullinan's class. Prior to that she had traveled to Ireland with her mother, and while there had danced at a feis. On that trip she also met Peter Bolton, the performer who had been in Chicago performing at the World's Fair in 1934. Pat Roche put Marge in contact with Bolton, and she was able to sit with him as he judged at the Father Mathew Feis in Dublin.[5]

67. 1959 Ireland Tour. Bottom: Mary Campbell, Michele Johnston, Maureen Daly, Joan O'Connor. Center: Frank Thornton, Mike Malone, Joanne Harnett, Mary Donnelley McDonagh, Johnny McGreevy, John Lavelle. Top: Johnny Woulfe, Jim Rudden, Beatrice Garrity, Margie Bartishell, Mary Jane Lucid, Paddy Gilhooley, Dennis Dennehy.

Bartishell had the foresight to bring instructors to Chicago who had the new "material" (choreography), and she offered workshops for select Chicago teachers. According to Jim Shea, who was an invited participant, teachers she brought to Chicago to conduct workshops included Annie Slattery from California, and John and Maureen McErlean from Belfast (via New York).[6] Mary Campbell Fahey remembers that Sean Constable, an All-Ireland dancer from Limerick, also held lessons for a select group of teachers that included herself, Mary Margaret Shea, and Marge Bartishell.[7] Constable was in Chicago for a period of time, and is listed as one of the judges for the 1955 Harp and Shamrock Feis. He also performed at various social functions and events around the city. Since Marge's dancers had the new style and new material, her classes became very popular and she attracted not only new students to Irish dance but transfers from many of long-established schools in the city.

Chicago Goes to Ireland

In 1959, Marge Bartishell and Dennis Dennehy participated in a performance tour of Ireland organized by Frank Thornton, a noted Chicago musician. The group worked with *Comhaltas Ceoltóirí Eireann,* the Musician's Association of Ireland, to plan the itinerary and schedule the venues. *Comhaltas* was organized in 1952 in Dublin and by the late 1950s the organization had grown to include one hundred and twenty branches and local music clubs throughout Ireland's thirty-two counties. The tour performed twenty-two sell-out performances in sixteen different counties, and visited all the popular locations in Ireland including Dublin, Belfast, Cork, Ennis, Clonmel, Listowel, Wexford, and Mullingar. The program included solo and group instrumental music, vocal selections, and a variety of dance pieces. The performers on the tour were fiddlers Jim Rudden, John McGreevy, and Mary McDonagh; accordian player John Lavelle; Michael Malone on piano; Patrick Gilhooley on drums; vocalists Joanne Harnett and Beatrice Garrity; and, dancers, Marge Bartishell, Mary Campbell, Joan O'Connor, Michelle Johnston, Maureen Daly, Mary Jane Lucid, Johnny Woulfe, and Dennis Dennehy. [Fig. 67]

The pieces included the expected repertoire, but interestingly, most were given unique titles. For instance, one of the features was "The Arches of Erin," a nine-hand reel. "Chicago Choice" was a four-hand jig performed by Maureen Daly, Patrick Gilhooley, Michelle Johnston, and John Woulfe.[8] The three-hand reel performed by Marge Bartishell, Dennis Dennehy, and Joan O'Connor was entitled, "The Crossroads." Another dance, a two-hand jig danced by Bartishell and Dennehy was called "Ireland's Glory," and the last number, "Margie's Pride," was a combined hornpipe. The remainder of the dance program included two set dances, "St. Patrick's Day" and "King of the Fairies," and a slip jig danced to "The Foxhunter."

One of the purposes of the trip was to highlight for those in Ireland how well the Irish in America had sustained the traditional music and dance of the homeland. From all accounts, the group was welcomed in Ireland and received wonderful reviews:

> Doherty's Hall, Drumshambo, was packed for the stage presentation by the Chicago Gaelic Concert Group, on Monday night

68. Marge Bartishell Dennehy and Dennis Dennehy.

week. In a very nicely arranged and balanced program, each of the Artistes distinguished him or herself in their own particular sphere of entertainment, while various exhibitions of Irish traditional Figure Dancing made a deep impression on the large audience. The vociferous applause and general manner in which the audience received the show, was, in itself, not alone, an indication and striking proof of the high standard of the presentation, which opened with the Irish National Anthem and closed with the American National Anthem.[9]

While in Belfast, the dancers met Anna McCoy, and in Dublin, they visited with Peter Bolton.[10]

69. The Dennehy Dancers. Back: Alana Dennis, Dennis Dennehy,
Michelle Johnston, Helen Ruf, James Thornton, Peggy Dineen, Danny Keogh,
Rose Virgo. Front: Patricia Walsh, Margaret McNamara, Brenda Dineen.

The Dennehy School

In 1961, Marge Bartishell and Dennis Dennehy were married. [Fig. 68]
Dennis became more consistently involved with teaching dance when
Marge was pregnant with their first child. From then on, they shared the role
of instructor, but Marge was always considered the creative force behind
their many artistic accomplishments. She had a gift for developing solo
steps, figure dances, and choreographies. Dennis commented that Marge
would sit at the table and use coins to figure out all the various, intricate
moves in the group dances she created. One of her first choreographies was
entitled "The Tri-Color," and consisted of nine dancers, three in green costumes, three in white, and three in orange.[11] The Dennehy Dancers were
making their mark not only in Chicago but across the Midwest and Canada
as they competed and won in regional feiseanna. [Figs. 69-70]

Through the 1970s, the Dennehy dancers continued to win at the
local, regional, and national competitions. As just mentioned, their chore-

70. Rose Virgo and Danny Keogh, Dennehy School.

ographies were always noteworthy. In the early 70s, before North America was divided into regions, the Dennehy dancers traveled to New York to compete at the National Oireachtas. When the regional Oireachtas became the qualifying event for the World Championships, the Dennehy dancers continued to be a strong school in the Midwest region.

New Competitions, New Teachers
Another significant event occurring in 1961 was the staging of the First Midwest Feis under the leadership of the Dennehy School of Dance. The event was held in Chicago at Pilsen Park, the same venue used for the Harp and Shamrock Feis that, since its inception in 1945, had been the only large-scale feis in Chicago, attracting dancers from around the country. By 1964, the Midwest Feis had moved to Polonia Grove at 47th and Archer Avenue, and the Harp and Shamrock Feis no longer existed.

By 1964, not only had the Chicago Feis changed sponsorship, but another fledgling feis had begun. A man named Tom Gleeson, under the banner of the Four Provinces of Ireland Club, sponsored a feis in the southern suburb of Harvey in August 1963. According to a *Tribune* article, "In addition to the Chicago area, dancers are coming from Connecticut, East St. Louis, Toronto, and Detroit."[12] In February of 1964, the club sponsored its second feis at St. Gabriel's Parish Auditorium.[13] Considering the size of the venue, it was not of the same scope as their first venture. This feis existed for only a few years and changed venue for each year of its existence. Interestingly, by 1966, they had changed the name from feis to "Festival of Irish Culture."[14]

In the late 1950s and early 60s, in addition to Bartishell-Dennehy, other new dance teachers emerged. Maureen Doyle started teaching in 1958, eventually taking over the classes of her teacher, Mary Shevlin McNamara. In 1960, Joe Cullinan decided to start teaching again, and together with Noreen Ring Travers, opened a school offering classes on the west and south sides of the city. Sheila Tully, Pat Roche's former student, started teaching on the west side, but quickly expanded her classes to include the western and northern suburbs as well. Lorraine Doran, one of Mary Campbell's dancers, began teaching on the south side.

In addition to the Chicago dancers who started teaching, a new arrival from Dublin, Nora Harling, also started a school on the north side.

Nora, a student of Ita Cadwell's, arrived in the city equipped with the new style of dance and with the type of new material that was catching everyone's attention at feiseanna and performances alike. She came from a well-established musical and dancing family who already had Chicago connections. Her brother, Sean Harling, a dancer himself who had been in the city for several years, was married to Marge Bartishell-Dennehy's sister. When the Chicago group was touring Ireland in 1959, Nora and her family met them. Before long, Nora's dancers were helping to set the standard for dance in Chicago, competing and winning in various championship events at regional feiseanna.[15]

Irish Dancing Teachers Association of North America (IDTANA)
In 1964, with the founding of a new organization—the Irish Dancing Teachers Association of North America (IDTANA)—significant changes in governance occurred in North America that would have long lasting effects on dance in Chicago. The dance teachers in Ireland had been organized for many years through *An Coimisiún le Rincí Gaelacha* (The Irish Dancing Commission) established in 1930 by the Gaelic League. In 1961, several dance teachers in the New York area who were already certified by the Commission, and, therefore, had strong ties with Ireland, decided to investigate the possibility of forming an organization that would be officially linked to the Commission in Dublin. Continued frustration with the tempo of the music and the standard of adjudication at feiseanna prompted this decision. In October 1961, in a letter written to the approximately ten certified teachers in North America at that time, Cyril McNiff argued that

> in order for any of us to receive any recognition for the particular style of Irish Dancing that we teach, it is necessary that we band together and form an organization similar to the Commission of Ireland. . . . [it should have] no connection with any Irish Dancing Teachers' Association in America.[16]

This group was trying to replace the IDTCA and create an association directly linked to Ireland and dedicated to the promotion of the new style of dancing. By 1964, the new organization was officially in place.

Chicagoans Marge and Dennis Dennehy were among the first members of this new group. With the establishment of IDTANA, the lines of communication were not only strengthened among North American teachers but were opened with dance teachers world-wide. As a result, exchanges and influences among various locations in North America and between North America and Ireland became the norm rather than isolated occurrences. In order to be in compliance with the Commission, more regulations and codification became a reality for the North American dance community.

One might wonder why, as stated by Pat Roche, Ireland was not interested in collaborating with America in the mid-1950s, but only one decade later was enthusiastically sanctioning the formation of IDTANA. One reason for this apparent change of heart could be that in Ireland, in the 1960s, dissatisfied teachers were starting a Dancing Teachers' and Adjudicators Congress, referred to as *An Comhdhail*. At that time, the Commission was still under the auspices of the Gaelic League, and some teachers felt that there should be more autonomy: an organization for teachers and by teachers. It can be argued that the Commission's new interest in establishing a strong foothold in North America was prompted, in part, by the perceived threat of *An Comhdhail,* whose members ultimately broke away from the Commission in 1969.[17]

Certifying Teachers

One of the early goals of the IDTANA was to increase the number of certified teachers and adjudicators in North America. In 1967, in an attempt to address this concern, exams were held in the United States, both in San Francisco and New York. Again, in 1969, the tests were held in New York. The success of these exams increased the numbers of qualified teachers and adjudicators, but the numbers still did not match the need, especially for adjudicators. Consequently, the Commission made a concession and allowed TCRGs (certified teachers) to judge competitions. This practice continued through the late 1970s after which time only ADCRGs (certified adjudicators) were allowed to judge.

With the guidance and leadership of Dennis Dennehy, exams were held in Chicago for the first time in 1972, and then again in 1976. Before the exams were held in Chicago, there were several dance teachers in the area who had traveled to Ireland to take the test, namely, Marge and Dennis Dennehy and Nora Harling in 1969, Mary Ellen Healy in 1970, and Peggy Roche Boyle early in 1972. Chicago teachers who received their TCRG at the first local exam included: Jim Shea, Mary Campbell Fahey, Sheila Tully Driscoll, Rose Virgo Kelly, and Alana Dennis Kelly. When the exams were held again in Chicago in 1976, even more Chicagoans received their TCRG. The cohort included: Lorraine Doran, Maureen Doyle, Maureen Ray Gilhooley, Geraldine Foy, Donna Killen, Kathleen Smyth, and Ann Murphy. At this same venue, several sat for the ADCRG exam as well. Included in that group were Peggy Roche Boyle, Mary Campbell Fahey, Maureen Doyle, Maureen Ray Gilhooley, Sheila Tully Driscoll, and Rose Virgo Kelly.[18]

Conducting the exams in the Midwest resulted in a significant increase in the number of certified teachers and adjudicators in the region. In time, being certified by the Commission in Dublin became a requirement for teaching Irish dance, not only in Chicago, but all over North America, since ultimately only certified teachers could enter students in feiseanna registered with the North American Feis Commission (NAFC).

In an effort to create more consistency among the numerous feiseanna being sponsored across the continent, the North American Feis Commission (NAFC) was established in 1968 to assist feis committees in planning their respective events. In the mid-1980s, non-certified teachers were still entering students in the Chicago Feis, but soon after only registered teachers could enter students. The effect of this rule was that one needed to pursue certification to be considered a full-fledged member of the Irish dance teachers' community and to be able to enter students in local feiseanna. Several Chicago teachers who, for various reasons, chose not to become certified ultimately closed their schools. Others who kept teaching chose performance events over competition. Some of those teachers who did not become certified but continued to teach included: Mary Shevlin McNamara, Noreen Kelly, Pat Moore, Jerry O'Laughlin, and Tony Weber-Brown. In 1986, Pat Roche was awarded an honorary TCRG by the Commission in recognition of his outstanding work as an Irish dancing master and diligent promoter of Irish dance, not only in Chicago but across the United States.

In 1989, the NAFC became officially affiliated with the Commission.

Thus the NAFC, the IDTANA, and the Commission—a triumvirate that, in effect, had been in existence for years before—was now officially established. The NAFC standardized feis rules, regulations, and the types of competitions offered, and also registered and scheduled all the various feiseanna across North America. Only teachers and adjudicators registered with IDTANA and the Commission could enter students and/or judge. The three groups worked together and became "the voice" of Irish dance in North America.

The Midwest Oireachtas

Another significant development that impacted the focus, quality, and style of Irish dance in Chicago was the creation of the National Oireachtas in 1969. The IDTANA's initial idea was to establish a national competition at which all the winners of the year's feiseanna could compete for a national title, with only students of registered teachers able to participate in this national event. This development coincided with the beginning of the World Championships in Ireland, and so it was decided that the National Oireachtas would be the qualifying event for the World Championships. The result was that dancers were now vying on a national level, and the quality of the steps, choreography, dance movements, and execution improved. The first National Oireachtas was held in Woodside, New York, over Thanksgiving weekend 1969. Through 1975, the event continued to be held in the New York area. Each year saw an increase in the number of competitors involved. [Fig. 71]

When in 1976 the Irish Dancing Commission divided North America into regions, incorporating regional qualifying events, the national venue was eliminated. According to Dennis Dennehy, the consistency in the standard of dance in Chicago suffered somewhat as a result.[19] Since Chicagoans no longer vied with dancers from all over North America, but only those from the Midwest region, the level of competition was to some extent diluted. Just as was the case in Pat Roche's time, Chicago teachers continued to feel that defeating the east coast dancers was the ultimate victory. With no national venue, the opportunities to vie with them were diminished. In 1981, when the Nationals were reinstated as an additional competitive venue, Dennehy feels that, across the board, the level of dance in Chicago improved. The Chicago dancers were once again able to compete against

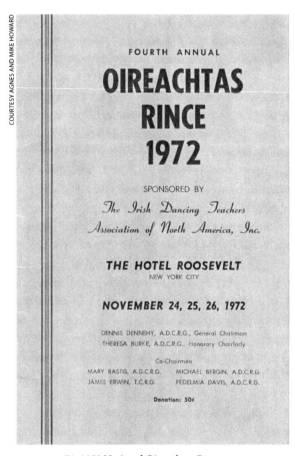

FOURTH ANNUAL

OIREACHTAS RINCE 1972

SPONSORED BY

The Irish Dancing Teachers Association of North America, Inc.

THE HOTEL ROOSEVELT
NEW YORK CITY

NOVEMBER 24, 25, 26, 1972

DENNIS DENNEHY, A.D.C.R.G., General Chairman
THERESA BURKE, A.D.C.R.G., Honorary Chairlady

Co-Chairmen
MARY BASTIS, A.D.C.R.G.   MICHAEL BERGIN, A.D.C.R.G.
JAMES ERWIN, T.C.R.G.   FEDELMIA DAVIS, A.D.C.R.G.

Donation: 50¢

71. 1972 National Oireachtas Program.

dancers from New York and Canada rather than just those from the Midwest region. The qualifying event for the Worlds was still the regional Oireachtas held each Thanksgiving weekend, but dancers vied for National titles each summer over the fourth of July weekend.

Chicago has hosted the Midwest Oireachtas on numerous occasions. For the first five years, the event basically alternated between Chicago and Cleveland. Then, in 1982, it was scheduled for Dayton, Ohio. Currently, the Oireachtas switches among various Midwestern cities, but Chicago is still a very popular venue for the event. When the Nationals were reinstated in 1981, Cleveland was the host city. The following years it was in

72. Michael Flatley with Pat Roche and Tommy Ryan, 1975.

Los Angeles, Toronto, Boston, Syracuse, and Chicago respectively. Presently, the Nationals are held annually at different venues across the United States and Canada. Over the last fifteen years, as the interest in Irish dancing has increased, there has been more variety in cities hosting the event. No longer is it confined to those eastern and midwestern cities that traditionally have had large Irish populations.

Competition has always been at the heart of Irish dance, and (with formal connection to the Commission, and the establishment of the World Championships) the goal of most Chicago dancers has been to win at the Worlds. Whereas in earlier days the goal was to defeat the east coast and Canadian dancers, now dancers want to defeat the Irish dancers at the Worlds. Chicago has the distinction of having the first North American dancer to win at the Worlds, namely Michael Flatley, who won the

73. Roche Boyle Adult Ceili Team: Patty Hastings, Kathy O'Connell,
Rita Ribakowski, Kate Disselhorst, Peggy O'Brien, Pat Gill,
Sue Connors, Patty O'Brien.

senior boys under seventeen competition in 1975. [Fig. 72] Presently, the
road to the Worlds means competing in numerous feiseanna throughout
the year, and qualifying for and placing at the regional Oireachtas. In addition, serious competitors would also compete at the Nationals, the All-
Ireland, and possibly other overseas championship competitions.

Adult Ceili Dancing
During the 1970s, as competitive dance was being shaped by the NAFC,
the IDTANA, and the Irish Dancing Commission, another phenomenon
in Irish dancing occurred in the Chicago area. Ceili dancing started to
become very popular and was attracting adult dancers into the ranks. John

Cullinane, in *Aspects of the History of Irish Ceili Dancing*, states that, "Ceili dancing came into prominence early in the 20th century and appears to have reached the height of its popularity in the 1930s-70s, after which it went into decline."[20] This may well have been the case in Ireland. But in Chicago, there was a definite ceili dance revival in the 1970s.

In Chicago, Peggy Roche Boyle, daughter of dance legend Pat Roche, started teaching adult ceili classes at Saint Xavier's College on the south side in the early 1970s. As part of the Roche School, she had been teaching young people for over a decade, but consciously decided to expand her teaching to include interested adults. Over the course of ten years, she taught classes each fall and spring term at the college. A few of the learners had taken some Irish dance lessons as youngsters, but the vast majority were trying Irish dance for the first time. [Fig. 73] With an increased interest in learning the various ceili dances, increased opportunities for performing also developed. By 1973 regularly scheduled ceili dances were being offered by the Emerald Music Club, under the leadership of Irish musician Noel Rice.[21] For many years these dances were held at the Swiss Club located at 2634 N. Laramie. Additionally, the newly formed Francis O'Neill Music Club offered dance lessons and ceili dances, and, in 1978, the Irish Musicians Association also began to sponsor regular ceilithe (pl. of ceili).[22]

Competitions also became part of the ceili dance experience. Prompted by the success of the Cleveland Feis in offering adult ceili competitions at the pre-feis party held the night before, the Chicago Feis also started to offer adult ceili competitions at their pre-feis celebration. Some of the ceili teams were new dancers from Roche-Boyle's ceili classes, others consisted of parents of dancers from the Dennehy School, while others were composed of veteran step dancers who had not danced for several years, but dusted off their dance shoes to get back on the floor. [Fig. 74] The winning team of the adult pre-feis ceili competition at the 1977 Chicago Feis included: Agnes Howard, Mike Howard, Sue Lewandowski, Helen Carroll, Peter Zografos, Eileen Watts, Jean Mullane, and Bridie Mulhern.[23] All team members worked on the feis committee, seven out of the eight were parents of a Dennehy dancer, and five out of the group were parents of dancers who ultimately became Chicago dance teachers. Agnes and Mike Howard fondly remember their time as members of the ceili

74. Dennehy Adult Ceili Team included veteran dancers.

team, dancing at many of the out-of-town feiseanna they attended with their children.[24] Roche-Boyle's teams consistently placed at the competitions, and at the 1980 pre-feis competition her teams won both first and second place.[25] Even though the adult ceili competitions are no longer part of the feis offerings, enthusiasm for ceili dancing still runs high in the city. The Irish American Heritage Center on the north side and Gaelic Park on the south side are among the locations where ceili and set dancing are regularly-scheduled events. John Cullinane's comment about the decline of interest in ceili dancing in 1970s Ireland certainly does not match the reality of what occurred in Chicago.

Chicago's First World Champion

Through the 1970s, the Dennehey dancers continued to win at local, regional, and national competitions. Their choreographies were always noteworthy. [Fig. 75] In the early 70s, before North America was divided into regions, the Dennehy dancers traveled to New York to compete at the National Oireachtas. When the regional Oireachtas became the qualifying event for the Worlds, the Dennehy dancers continued to be a strong school in the Midwest region.

   One of the star pupils of the Dennehy School, Michael Flatley, has the distinction of being the first North American to win at the Worlds. [Fig. 76]

75. Dennehy's "Lord of the Dance," 1976.

Flatley started lessons at the relatively late age of eleven; however, he proved to be a natural. He was soon vying at the national level for titles, and in 1973, at the age of fifteen, won first place at the National Oireachtas. When he traveled to the Worlds the next spring, he was disappointed to place only fourth in his competition. But after additional training in Ireland with Kevin Massey, he returned to the Worlds in 1975 and took first in his age group.[26] Unquestionably, Flatley is a unique talent, and even though much of his success is due to his own personal drive and ability, being in Chicago provided him with an environment that nurtured his extraordinary talent. By 1978 he opened his own dance school, and because of his reputation and talent, many dancers from the more established schools transferred to Flatley. At the Chicago Feis in June 1979, Flatley's dancers placed either first, second, or third in six out of the eight championship categories.[27] At the Midwest Oireachtas held in Chicago in November 1980, Flatley's students placed either first, second, or third in eight out of the eighteen age groups. And in three of those age groups, two of his dancers were in the top places.[28]

IRISH AMERICAN NEWS JULY 1978

76. Michael Flatley, 1978.

77. Flatley's Ceili 16-18 Band, Midwest Fleadh Cheoil, 1980. Front: Bernadette Dillon, Mary Treacy, Tom Molloy, Eileen Mulhern, Eileen Cloonan. Back: Steve Trant, Jim Smith, Michael Flatley (instructor), Michael Barry, Jim Gillespie.

Flatley not only taught dance, but also taught music. He had won the All-Ireland on the concert flute in 1975, and the following year he won on the wooden flute. In *The Irish American News* of May 1980, Flatley is pictured with two of his winning ceili bands which had competed at the Midwest Fleadh Cheoil the month before.[29] Many of the young musicians were also his dance students. [Figs. 77-78] Flatley was the center of attraction during the 1970s as a champion dancer and musician, and then as a teacher. However, compared to others, his tenure as a dance teacher was short-lived. By 1986, on the Official List of Registered Teachers and Adjudicators published by the Irish Dancing Commission, Flatley was registered as an inactive TCRG without a school.

78. Flatley's Ceili 11-14 Band, Midwest Fleadh Cheoil, 1980. Front: Jim Coyle,
Pat Cloonan, Sheila Coyle, Colleen Mulhern, Kevin Barry, Tom Coyle.
Back: Michael Flatley (instructor), John Williams, Pat Coyle, Tim Duggan.

Chicago's Irish Day

After the Harp and Shamrock Feis was discontinued, and both the Midwest Feis and the short-lived Gaelic Arts Association Feis had ceased, the Chicago Feis Committee continued to sponsor their annual feis at various locations around the Chicago area from the mid-1970s. The venues at which these feiseanna were held included: Angel Guardian on the north side, McCormick Place Inn, the Northlake Hotel, the Du Page County Fairgrounds, and, finally, Gaelic Park on the far south side of the metro area. Dancers could be assured that there would be at least one major competition held each year in Chicago.

In 1982, the competitive opportunities expanded with the creation of the Illinois Invitational Feis sponsored by the Sheila Tully School. The event was held on the grounds of Maryville Academy located on the northwest side of the metro area. The event ended up being held each year in June, on Father's Day. For many years the Chicago Feis was held on the day before, so out-of-town dancers could easily attend both feiseanna during the same weekend. At that time, Chicago dancers were grateful for two competitive opportunities in the metropolitan area. Things have certainly changed since then. Nowadays feiseanna are much more numerous in the Chicago area, with six currently listed on the NAFC calendar. The events are scheduled year round, not just during the summer months as had traditionally been the case. Additionally, there are five feiseanna scheduled in nearby Milwaukee, one in Madison, Wisconsin, and another in South Bend, Indiana, all of which are easily accessible to Chicago dancers. The opportunities for competition have increased tremendously, and competition continues to be the life blood of Irish dance.

Even though competition continues to be the driving force in Irish dance, performance at social clubs, commercial establishments, Catholic schools and parishes, and festivals have always provided numerous venues for Irish dancers to spotlight their art for the general public. In the late 1970s, the Lady Day in Harvest Festival, traditionally celebrated around 15 August, was revived in Chicago. Billed as "Irish Family Day," the event was scheduled for 15 August 1977 at the Chicago Amphitheater. As described in an article in the *Irish American News*, "The purpose of this get together is to show the strength of the Irish, and to present a great panorama of the faith and the joy and the talent of the Irish."[30] In conjunction with the event, Mayor Michael Bilandic declared that August 15th would be "Irish Day" in the city of Chicago. The dancing portion of the entertainment was coordinated by veteran Irish dance teacher, Mae Kennedy Kane, and according to the *Irish American News*, twenty-two Irish dance schools were scheduled to perform.[31] The proceeds of the event were to benefit the Irish American Heritage Center building fund. Various Irish clubs in Chicago combined to sponsor the celebration, with Tommy Ryan of the Shannon Rovers and Dan Burke of the Emerald Society as co-chairmen.

79. Maureen Harling's Dancers: Front: Colleen O'Shea, Danny O'Shea, Michael O'Shea, Katie O'Shea. Back: Jodie Houlihan, Jacqueline Collins, Laurie Miller, Kay Sopron, Mary Ann McInerney, Julie Ann Botwinski, Colleen Brogan.

The success of the event prompted the committee to schedule another celebration for the following year. Navy Pier was chosen as the new site for the 20 August 1978 gathering. Co-chairs were Bob Dwyer of the Emerald Society and Liam O'Breen of the Gaelic Athletic Association. Once again, Mae Kennedy Kane was the coordinator of the dancing program, and according to the *Irish American News,* seven dance schools were involved.[32] "Irish Family Day" continued to be held at Navy Pier for several more years; then, in 1982, it moved to Hawthorne Race Course in Cicero, and was extended as a two-day event. The following year, 1983, it was again held at the race track as a two-day celebration. For seven consecutive years, "Irish Family Day" created a performance venue for the Irish dancers in Chicago. The celebration provided great exposure for the dancers and a wonderful performance opportunity for those teachers who had opted not to pursue the TCRG and who were becoming less involved with competition. Unfortunately, for a variety of reasons, chiefly the inception of Milwaukee Irish Fest in 1981, "Irish Family Day" in Chicago ceased after 1983.

A New Generation

Another young, accomplished dancer who opened a school during this time was Maureen Harling. She started teaching in 1976, and received her TCRG in Ireland in the spring of 1980.[33] Harling was strongly rooted in the tradition of Irish dance. She was the niece of Marge and Dennis Dennehy, and also of Nora Harling Gardner, all of whom directed champion-producing schools. Her father, Sean Harling, had also been an active Irish dancer in his day. [Fig. 79]

The early 1980s witnessed a new generation of teachers emerging onto the Irish dance scene in Chicago. Among the teachers who opened or joined existing schools during the 1980s were: Jim McGing and Mark Howard who opened the McGing-Howard school in 1980; brother and sister, Mary and Paul Mayer; Kathy Carroll and Ann Fegan who opened Cross Keys; Barbara McNulty; Valerie Whelan; brother and sister, Mary Alice and Michael Mullane; and, Kathy Dennehy, the daughter of Marge and Dennis Dennehy. All of these new teachers had been Dennehy dancers. It is indeed a tribute to the Dennehy School to have trained so many dancers who ultimately became dance teachers themselves.

By 1983, the McGing-Howard School had split; Mark Howard had opened the Trinity Academy and Jim McGing had created the McGing School. All of these new teachers ultimately received their TCRG and became active in the Irish Dance Teachers Association of Mid-America (ID-TAMA), the regional teachers' organization, and the IDTANA, the national organization. In addition to the Chicago natives who opened schools, in 1988 Ann Lavin Cassidy was listed as a TCRG in Chicago. A native of Ireland, who was also trained there, Lavin Cassidy's school has continued to produce champion dancers in Chicago throughout the years. With the retirement of Nora Harling Gardner, Ann Lavin Cassidy was the only Irish-born dance teacher actively teaching in Chicago.

By 1990, Irish dance was witnessing a steady increase in the numbers of certified teachers. Chicago dance schools consistently sent students to the regional Oireachtas, the Nationals, and the Worlds, and Chicago dancers were making a name for themselves at both national and international competitions. Through the various teachers' organizations, the NAFC, and the Irish Dancing Commission in Dublin, dancing had become more organized and codified. The pioneers of Irish dance in

Chicago, people like Dan Ryan, James Coleman, John Ryan, and John Mc-Namara would have been duly impressed with the outcome of their early work. With their enthusiasm and diligence, those men laid the foundations, and subsequent leaders, like Pat Roche and Marge and Dennis Dennehy, were able to strengthen the tradition while expanding the boundaries. Thanks to all their work, Chicago continued (and does still) to be an acknowledged stronghold of Irish dance.

CHAPTER 5

Staging New Traditions: Beyond Competition

During the twentieth century, Irish dance in Chicago evolved in scope and structure. From a small nucleus of native-born Irish who knew a few steps and performed them only occasionally—and then only at private parties or gatherings—Irish dance developed into an organized, public, and popular activity. From an activity that included only adults, it changed into one that was geared primarily to young people. From an activity that was performed for the enjoyment of the Irish community, it expanded its audience to include residents of the city of Chicago, the United States, and ultimately, the world.

Michael Flatley

During the twentieth century, Irish dance moved from an expression of ethnic pride to an innovative dance form. The years 1995-2005 will go down in Irish dance history as the decade of the spectacular stage shows, extravaganzas with Irish dance and music as the medium. Shows like *Riverdance, Lord of the Dance, Feet of Flames,* and *Celtic Tiger* have invaded not only American popular culture but global culture as well. The lure of commercial success also spawned such second-tier touring shows as *Spirit of the Dance* and *The Spirit of Ireland.* This cultural entertainment phenomenon is closely linked to Chicago native Michael Flatley, the original star of *Riverdance* who was responsible for most of the creative dance material in the full production. Encouraged by the enthusiastic reception of the seven-minute Riverdance interval piece staged for the 1991 Eurovision song contest, almost overnight entrepreneurs and artists devised the full stage production. Flatley was at the center of it all.

Before *Riverdance,* Flatley had toured extensively with the traditional Irish music group, the Chieftains, appearing at venues that included New York's Carnegie Hall and London's Royal Albert Hall. Additionally, Flatley received numerous awards and recognitions for his work. Among others, he received the National Endowment for the Arts Heritage Fellowship in 1988, and was named a Living Treasure by the National Geographic Society in 1991.

After a disagreement over creative control with the *Riverdance* producers, Flatley abruptly separated from the troupe and quickly went on to create and star in his own production, *Lord of the Dance,* which opened in Dublin in July 1996. The production was extremely successful, touring world-wide, and continues to tour at the present time. As Flatley was touring the U.S. with the show, he was asked to appear at the 1997 Academy Awards, even though *Lord of the Dance* had no connection to the film industry. Flatley and his dancers wowed the audience with their performance, and created another first—Irish dancing at the Academy Awards. Sid Smith, art critic for the *Chicago Tribune,* said of Flatley that:

> The story behind Lord of the Dance is both the grueling rags to riches story of Flatley himself and the even larger, amazing saga of a folk art's journey from pastime to box-office bonanza. Flatley is not the only star in the galaxy but he is arguably the brightest, hottest, fastest and most combustible. [1]

Even though Flatley left *Riverdance* very early in the life of the touring show, his name will always be linked with it. When one hears the name Riverdance, one immediately thinks of Michael Flatley not only because of the choreography that he created for the show, but also because of his dynamic performances in the lead role.[2] In a 1997 *Los Angeles Times* interview, it was clear that Flatley

> sees himself as the benevolent liberator of Irish dance: "All I know is that one day I went to Ireland and everyone was dancing like this"— he holds his arms rigidly at his sides—"and the next day we were headlines all over the world. I must have done something right."[3]

The popularity of *Lord of the Dance* is astounding. In April 1997 it was reported that for video sales, "while it took 'Riverdance' one year to sell one million videos, it took 'Lord of the Dance' only 12 weeks to sell 1.5 million."[4]

However, the huge popularity with the general public was not consistently matched by the critics. For example, David Dougill, in *The Sunday Times* (London), wrote that the troupe was technically brilliant, but that

> The nub of the problem is the choreography, and the intrinsic limitations of the Irish dancing (almost all for the feet, leaving the upper body looking spare) as a medium for dance-drama.... [as] thrilling as the big showpiece numbers are, the dance vocabulary is very repetitive. Not that this reservation will bother Flatley's fans one jot.[5]

In a review in the *Chicago Sun-Times,* Lynn Voedisch wrote that

> Flatley is, without any doubt, a spellbinding dancer. With perfect control of every muscle, every mannerism, Flatley drills home searing footwork tapping out rhythms that nearly stop your heart. His carriage is perfect, his delivery pure and sure. When he kicks to the rafters or sails in an arcing leap, Flatley can do absolutely no wrong. So we forgive him excesses, no matter how great.... It's an ego trip—and it's a lot of fun.[6]

His latest creation, *Celtic Tiger,* opened in New York's Madison Square Garden in September 2006. In late October he was forced to cancel his thirty-four city North American tour because of medical problems. The reviews of his newest work were not particularly positive: "Mr. Flatley is the consummate showman, and 'Celtic Tiger' is more spectacle than dance."[7] This seems to be a typical response to Flatley's work by the dance world. They feel he has sacrificed art for box office revenues. Dance critic Mindy Aloff thought that "Flatley's original ideas for 'Riverdance' . . . were pathbreaking for commercial entertainment and for Irish dancing as well.... [He] is one of the true dance geniuses of our time."[8] The problem as Aloff sees it is that "After 'Riverdance' Flatley seems to have decided to pursue box office for its own sake.... He remains a great technician, even a great dancer. However, in my view, he's no longer an artist. Once, he was."[9] The critic for the *Irish Times,* Michael Seaver, had a problem with the image of Ireland presented in *Celtic*

Tiger: He said, "We no longer cling to the post-colonial victim status that is put forward in 'Celtic Tiger.' Neither do we think that the only route of escape from poverty and oppression is to go to America!—another subtext in these shows."[10]

Regardless of the critical response to Flatley's recent work, audiences still pack arenas worldwide to see his shows. According to the *San Diego Union Tribune,* he is said to be worth $620 million, and his legs insured for $20 million each.[11] Flatley moved from champion Irish dancer to performer to superstar using Irish dance as his artistic medium. According to a 2008 article in the *Irish Daily Mirror,* "Super-hoofer Michael Flatley will become 'Lord of the Loot' earning more than any other performer this year —even if he doesn't set foot on stage."[12] The commercial success of his dance enterprises is truly astounding.

Trinity Irish Dance Company

While Flatley has continued to make incredible profits, less commercially driven groups have continued to investigate new and exciting possibilities in Irish dance. Most notably, the nonprofit, Chicago-based Trinity Irish Dance Company has been choreographing and commissioning works described as "progressive" Irish dance since 1990, long before *Riverdance* or *Lord of the Dance* were created and produced. Trinity's focus is the art rather than the profit. A problem which was becoming evident during the last decades of the twentieth century was that Irish dancing was primarily confined to competition, and its reach and impact was confined to those who were involved with dance schools competing on a national and international level. The Irish dancing world was extremely parochial. The incredible technical proficiency, extensive repertoire, and creative accomplishments attained by many dancers had no where to go. A few dancers, such as Michael Flatley, gained some exposure by touring with music groups like the Chieftains, but there were few opportunities for Irish dancers to continue dancing after retiring from competition.

The Trinity Irish Dance Company, formed in Chicago in 1990 by Mark Howard, was a response to this dilemma. Howard, a Chicagoan, had been trained at the Dennehy School of Irish Dance and had successfully started his own dance academy. After receiving recognition by winning at the World Championships in Ireland in the dance drama category, which al-

80. Trinity Academy Dance Drama Team visiting Ireland for the Worlds, 1987.

lows for more creativity than other competitive categories, and by multiple appearances on NBC's *The Tonight Show with Johnny Carson* and other national television programs, Howard was inspired to turn Irish dance into a performance art. [Figs. 80-81] He began choreographing more for performances than competition with its constricting regulations. He had always been trying to push the confining boundaries established for competition, and is proud of the fact that his dance teams were disqualified more than once for daring to be different.[13]

With the founding of the company, Howard's mission was to "push the boundaries" and "create life after competitive dancing." As noted in *Irish Dancing Magazine*, "He began infusing Irish dance with overtones of ballet and modern, African, East Indian, Spanish, and tap, and he started to get noticed."[14] As Howard himself explains, "We've taken up an ethnic craft and reintroduced it as an art-form, always evolving and expanding."[15]

It is important to emphasize that Trinity was working on progressive Irish dance several years before the stage show *Riverdance* achieved international acclaim. The impetus behind *Riverdance* was always commercial, as opposed to Trinity's desire to promote the art form and have Irish dance accepted as a legitimate and classical art form by the dance

81. Mark Howard and Johnny Carson, Tonight Show 1988.

world. It is also interesting to note that both Howard and Flatley, the two dancers who have had the most creative impact on Irish dance outside the world of competition, are both from Chicago and are both alums of the Dennehy School. In reference to the fact that he is not from Ireland, Mark Howard says that he doubts he would be a leader in progressive Irish dance if he had been born and raised there. He says, "These traditional steps that were in my head and learned as a child, were also mixed with all this other stimuli, living in an urban environment like Chicago and watching things like MTV . . . What we gave back was a different take on the tradition. It was uniquely an Irish American viewpoint"[16]

The critical reactions to Trinity's work have been mixed. They made their New York debut at the Joyce in August 1997. Writing in the *New York Times,* Jennifer Dunning, stated that

Mr. Howard is faced with a familiar problem in Irish folk dance programs, however. There is not a lot of variety to the forms, But "progressive Irish dance," as Mr. Howard puts it, often looks impoverished when compared with the exciting purity of the traditional forms . . . . Mr. Howard and his colleagues are to be commended for trying to extend the form, but the more traditional dances like "Blackthorn," "Step About," "Johnny," and "The Dawn" win hands down.[17]

The writer definitely preferred the "tried and true" Irish dances to those that stretched the usual repertoire. Most of the dancers involved in the company had little dance training other than Irish, so trying new techniques was challenging for them.

An article that appeared in the November 1997 issue of *Dance Magazine* provided more pointedly negative comments:

Despite the clarity of its footwork, the corps of girl goddesses seemed meant to serve merely as happy Celtic bodies in garish outfits. They tapped, spun, grinned, and changed costumes for dances that ranged from straightforward baubles (Step About, 1991) to confused melodramas (the premiers of Bansidhe and The Mollies).[18]

By August of 1999 the reviews had mellowed a bit. In an article in the *Christian Science Monitor,* M. S. Mason notes that:

Many Americans have seen Riverdance on TV or in the theater, and that commercialized, high-tech entertainment has given Irish step-dancing a boost. But the real art of the dance may lie elsewhere—in a company like Trinity that has made a genuine effort to place itself in the high art, rather than commercial venues.[19]

The writer gives credit to Trinity for its creativity and its emphasis on experimenting with dance as opposed to merely relying on the wizardry of technical production. Mason comments that Howard "has taken his company in another direction, away from theatrical spectacle and toward innovative theatre pieces," and alludes to the fact that Irish dancers need to move beyond craft to a new expression, to creativity.[20] Again, the challenge is to retain the core culture but allow for new expressions.

Innovation in Irish Dance

The question that often arises in response to these new and varied manifestations of Irish dance is: has the core of this ethnic tradition been compromised? Or, are all these manifestations an inevitable and healthy development? Traditionally, competition has been the driving force behind new developments in Irish dance. New moves were integrated into steps performed by dancers at the championship level. The moves that are part of the winners' repertoires then begin to appear in other dancers' pieces. Irish dancers truly believe in the adage, "imitation is the sincerest form of flattery." As new moves become part of the Irish dancing vernacular, questions sometimes arise regarding the traditional aspects of the art form. How closely do the new movements need to adhere to "the tradition" in order to be considered Irish dancing?

A close look at the history of Irish dance points out that Irish dancing has always been influenced by other dance traditions. John Cullinane, who has done extensive research on the history of Irish dance, comments that "the similarity between the Scottish and Irish dances as early as 1549 is significant."[21] It was the Normans who are credited with introducing round dances to Ireland. The French quadrilles, in their formation and figures, are extremely similar to Irish sets and ceili dances. Cullinane states:

It is my belief that our set dances were originally quadrilles that arrived in Ireland either directly from France or indirectly via England and having arrived here, use was made of the existing Irish music in reel and jig time . . . .What is important and what is the only important thing is that by now we have made such dances truly Irish."[22]

Gearóid Ó hAllmhuráin claims that reels and hornpipes did not arrive in Ireland until the end of the eighteenth century:

the reel in its present form was imported from Scotland . . . Similarly, the modern hornpipe was probably imported from England around the same period. It was popular as a stage act in the English theatre and was usually performed in between acts and at the close of plays."[23]

Thus, many of the dances which constitute the foundation of Irish dance were most likely imported, adapted, and ultimately became "the tradition."

This point is also made by Helen Brennan:

In many areas of Britain such as Lancashire, Cumbria, Norfolk, Suffolk, Devon and the Western Isles and east coast of Scotland, we find evidence of "stepping" which contains elements similar to and in some cases identical to the Irish steps. The close connections between, for example, Ireland and Lancashire in the form of Irish migrant labour in the cotton mills would point to the likelihood of an input by these workers into the dance of their temporary home abroad as well as the possibility that they carried steps home with them.[24]

During the first days of the Gaelic League and into the first days of the Irish Republic, these facts were difficult for many native Irish to accept. For them, Irish dancing was part of the cultural revival, a revival that emphasized the country's Gaelic roots, shunned Anglo influences, and strengthened the movement to free Ireland from British subjugation. To insinuate that Irish dances were imported from England was anathema to the nationalists. Brennan points out that the heated debates that took place in the early 1900s about the authenticity of certain Irish dances basically constituted a "cultural civil war with dance as the arena of combat."[25] Because dance was being considered in the context of a colonial and then post-colonial people, the need to stress the dances as authentic and part of the pure Gaelic tradition became paramount. Irish dancing was one of a variety of cultural symbols used by political nationalists to instill a sense of ethnic pride, not only in Ireland but also in the United States. Because of this history, questions of authenticity and genuine tradition are still part of the conversations and controversies confronting Irish dance today.

While interviewing two of Pat Roche's dancers who took lessons from him in Chicago in the late 1930s and early 40s, they mentioned that after watching the Lithuanian dancers at one of the national folk festivals in which they performed, they were so intrigued by a few of the figures they observed that they decided to incorporate a couple of the moves into their three-hand reel.[26] Ethnic dance boundaries were fluid back them, and continue to be so today.

Solo step dances first appeared on the Irish landscape during the last half of the eighteenth century, created by the traveling dancing masters who followed specified circuits through the countryside, staying for about a six week period in each location before moving on. The reputation of these dancing masters was based not only on their ability to teach but also on their ability to invent new steps.[27] Even today the reputation of teachers is based in part on their ability create new material, i.e. to choreograph new steps. The continual creation of new steps has always been an important characteristic of Irish dances both in the present and historically. Irish dance, then, has always borrowed from and been influenced by other traditions, it has always involved the creation of new steps and material, and it has always managed to adapt these varied ingredients into something "Irish." Even though the die-hard nationalists would like to take exception to this reality, the fact remains that there is no such thing as a "pure" Irish tradition.

Trinity and Sean Curran

Sean Curran was commissioned to create three pieces for Trinity Irish Dance Company. In general, the critiques of Curran's work were positive and his contributions to Trinity's program greatly enhanced their repertoire. Having a background in Irish dance certainly helped Curran connect with the company. His first piece, "Curran Event," was mentioned in the *New York Times* in March 2000. Jack Anderson described it as "unusually bouncy choreography . . . Rhythmic patterns were often deliberately irregular and the dancers helped make their own music by slapping their bodies and those of the companions."[28]

Tobi Tobias, in *New York Magazine* (2001), makes several negative comments about the troupe, but he has positive remarks about Curran's work:

The most creative departure from tradition was achieved by Sean Curran (a postmodern dancer and choreographer with a background in step dancing). His Curran Event co-opts related rhythmic forms like body percussion to create patterns intricate enough to

TRINITY IRISH DANCE COMPANY

82. Curran Event, 2000.

keep the eye alert and the pulse throbbing in response.[29] [Fig. 82]

Tobias identifies the body percussion as being from another tradition, as non-Irish movement. However, Breandan Breathnach mentions the Clap Dance, an old Irish dance, which incorporated this same type of action:

> It was performed by two people who sat together or stood opposite each other. They started the performance by striking their own knees with the palms of their hands. Then they struck their partner's hands with their own in patterned combinations of movements.[30]

So, something that at first appears to be new and foreign to Irish dance, does, in fact, have roots in Irish cultural dance history.

In *Dance Magazine* (June 2001), Martha Ullman West acknowledges that Trinity is about Irish tradition but also about stretching it and fusing it with other styles. She feels that Sean Curran makes a "healthy stab at

131

manipulating the strictly codified form," but she continues by stating, "It's not quite successful: Charlies's Angels with a revolutionary edge."[31] More praise for Curran's contributions to Trinity came from Jack Anderson writing in the *New York Times* in March 2002:

> One of Mr. Howard's brightest ideas of recent seasons was to bring Sean Curran as guest choreographer. Although Mr. Curran is a modern dancer, he was originally trained in Irish dancing, and he knows how to blend forms. His new "Jump, Jive, and Jig" borrows steps from swing and jitterbug dancing.[32]

Similar feelings were expressed by Jennie Schulman writing in *Backstage*:

> It wasn't until choreographer Sean Curran's work entered the scene that we began to see true expansive forms. His 'Jump, Jive, and Jig,' which was given its New York premier, justified the claim that it 'combines elements of jitterbug, swing, and disco with the virtuosity and speed of solo and social Irish dance.' And does Curran's choreography ever deliver![33]

When commenting on "Curran Event" the writer is again extremely positive, stating that "Curran again delivered startling originality. There were prime examples of widely spread out, dazzling choreographic patterns, which we had never seen previously in other Celtic companies."[34]

During its 2004 fall touring season, Trinity introduced Curran's third commissioned choreography entitled, "Goddess." Tom Strini reviewed the piece in the *Milwaukee Journal Sentinel*:

> The heartening news came from guest choreographer Sean Curran, who makes a strong case for Irish dance as a concert art with someplace still to go . . . Curran turns to India in 'Goddess' a gorgeous compare-and-contrast number that draws on Bharata Natyam, classical temple dancing. . . . Just by taking the same old hard-shoe steps and subjecting them to Indian rhythm, Curran respects the tradition even as he casts it in a whole new light. The flowing Indian gestures above those Irish feet complement rather than clash.[35]

Trinity has truly benefitted from Curran's collaborative efforts. His work has been positively received by the critics and he seems able to provide a creative approach to Irish dance, blending it with other traditions, but keeping an Irish core. By continuing to invite creative choreographers to work with the company, Trinity will be more likely to insure variety while continuing its stated mission. Even though some Irish dancing traditionalists might question Trinity's work, Irish dancing has always been influenced by importation, imitation, and invention.

In the final analysis, Mark Howard's Trinity Irish Dance Company and all Michael Flatley's commercial productions have positively impacted Irish dance. These have been healthy developments, for as the new has been investigated, the old has been rediscovered. While there has been a staggering increase in the number of people involved in competitive Irish dance, there is also a renewed interest in the old styles of Irish dance. At venues around the world, workshops in the more traditional solo dances and styles are commonplace. There has also been an explosion of interest in traditional Irish set dancing. Regular set dancing classes and sessions crowd the Irish activities calendars in Chicago as well as other urban areas. The almost extinct solo tradition known as *sean-nós* is making a healthy comeback as well. Adults are either rediscovering or learning these dances for the first time. All of these examples indicate that the core of this ethnic dance tradition has definitely not been compromised. It may in fact have been strengthened by the innovations of contemporary choreographers. Through his Trinity Irish Dance Company, Howard is successfully providing a future for Irish dance in the twenty-first century. Traditions are not static but ever evolving. In order for Irish dance to remain vibrant, it must continue to evolve and carve out new traditions while celebrating the old. And, if history continues to repeat itself, the city of Chicago will continue to retain its place as a creative and significant center of Irish dance.

A Brief Overview of Irish Dance

T he history of Irish dancing in general is somewhat sketchy in that, before the sixteenth century, there are only a few vague references to dancing found in the literature. However, the lack of written documentation does not necessarily mean that dancing was not a part of the life of the early Irish. As John Cullinane points out, "One must keep in mind the fact that much of the early Irish literature was destroyed at a later date due to English suppression."[1] During the sixteenth and seventeenth centuries there were a number of passing references to Irish dance found in the Anglo-Irish and English literature of the time, but these were written by those who knew little about dance and even less about Irish dance.[2] It is not until the eighteenth century that Irish dance in the literature begins to evince the form that is recognizable today.

Irish dance can be categorized into solo dances and group dances. Solo dances are also referred to as "step dances" because the dancer performs individual steps that are strung together to make whole dances. The basic step dances are the jig, reel, and hornpipe. It is this canon of step dances that gives traditional Irish dancing its unique character. Regarding their development Breandan Breathnach states that "The last quarter of the eighteenth century seems the most likely period for their invention, and there can be little doubt we owe their existence to the dancing masters."[3]

The dancing master became a part of the Irish landscape as he traveled from village to village teaching dancing to the cottiers' (tenant farmers') children. Each dancing master had his own district and he would travel a regular circuit. The dancing master's arrival was met with great joy, as it signaled several weeks of music and dancing in the village. He was a flamboyant fellow with an unmistakable appearance:

Caroline hat, swallow-tail coat and tight knee-breeches, white stockings and turn-pumps, cane with a silver head and silk tassel—thus accoutered the dancing master was obviously a cut above the wandering piper or fiddler. He was a person to be treated with due deference by his pupils. Good carriage and deportment were his by profession. He considered himself a gentleman, conducted himself as one, and endeavoured to instil this spirit into his best pupils.[4]

The dancing master's reputation was built not only on his skill as a dancer, but on also his ability to teach as well as his talent to invent and choreograph new steps.

A "set dance" is another type of solo dance in which the dancer performs to a specific traditional tune. These dances are usually more intricate and require more advanced training. These set dances were the creations of individual dancing masters. Five of the traditional set dances that appeared regularly on Irish dance programs in Chicago at the beginning of the twentieth century, and are therefore mentioned frequently in this study, are: *The Blackbird, The Job of Journeywork, The Garden of Daisies, The Humors of Bandon,* and *St. Patrick's Day.*

Step dancing requires agility, precision, and intricate footwork. The dance steps progress in technical difficulty so that students start with a beginner reel and jig, followed by an intermediate level reel and jig, followed by the treble jig and hornpipe that require movements called shuffles or batters, movements similar to those seen in American tap dance. As dancers become more proficient, more complicated versions of the dances are learned.

Group dances include figure dances, ceili dances, and country set dances. These dances do not require the intricate footwork of the solo dances. When describing the work of the dancing master, Brendan Breathnach comments:

> The less gifted and more numerous members of the company found an outlet for their high spirits in the round or group dances, which, it is said, were devised by the dancing masters to maintain the interest of their less ardent pupils and afford couples an opportunity for colloguing.[5]

After learning a few basic movements such as the promenade and side step, dancers can easily learn a variety of group dances.

The figure dances are probably the most challenging in this category. They are longer, have little repetition and, consequently, there is more to remember. Also the figures themselves (i.e., movement patterns and shapes) that the dancers create by dancing around and among each other are a bit more complicated. Ceili dances tend to be very repetitive, and are thus easier for the more casual Irish dancer to perform. Usually there are three or four movements that are continually repeated. The country dances (called "sets") are probably the least intricate, and yet they do have a style all their own. The sets are danced by either four or eight dancers. Many are identified by the geographic location in Ireland in which they were popular, i.e., the Kerry set, the Clare set, the Mayo set, etc..

In order to be able to perform them correctly, step dances and most figure dances require continued instruction from a dance teacher. For Irish step dancing to develop and thrive in a community it is necessary to have a dancing master or qualified teacher involved and regular lessons offered. This fact is central to the story of the development and promotion of Irish dancing in Chicago, an American location where dancing masters from Ireland began to appear in the late nineteenth century.

The History of Irish Dance Costume in Chicago

A s Irish dance evolved in Chicago, both stylistically and organizationally, the dance costumes, shoes, and accessories evolved as well. Unfortunately, there is little specific information available about the type of dance shoe worn by those who were performing in Chicago at the beginning of the twentieth century. From the few available photos, it appears that they did not wear any special type of footwear. According to John Cullinane, as late as 1924, the dancers in Belfast and Cork, even when performing in dance competitions, were still wearing the "traditionally accepted light everyday walking shoes."[6]

Shoes

The Roche dancers who performed at the Irish Village at the Century of Progress in 1934 stated that they wore taps on their shoes.[7] This information is surprising because an important feature of competitive Irish dancing has always been an articulated prohibition against metal taps on dancing shoes. Instead, an extra piece of leather was put on the tip of the shoe and a few nails were added to provide sound. Hearing the beat of the dance step has always been an important characteristic of certain Irish dances like the hornpipe and jig, so wearing taps, which were both popular and available in the U.S. during the 1930s, makes sense. However, Roche's dancers discontinued the use of metal taps by the late 1930s. Mae Kennedy Kane, on the other hand, who taught other types of dancing as well as Irish, kept them. By the 1950s, her dancers were unique among Irish dancers in Chicago in that they were the only ones who wore taps on their shoes for performances.

Possibly, the guidelines and rules developed after the founding of the Irish Dancing Commission in 1931 affected the type of shoe worn by most dancers in Chicago. Even though the U.S. was not officially connected

83. Roche Dancers: Mary Shevlin, Peggy Mulvihill, Eileen Ring,
Nancy O'Malley, Anne Heneghan, Mary Heneghan.

with the Commission at that time, Pat Roche frequently mentioned that
he wanted to develop a stronger connection with Ireland and wanted to
be aware of what was happening with the dance in Ireland in order to
maintain the authenticity of his work and strengthen the quality of dance
in Chicago and across the United States.[8] Since Bolton and Danaher were
in Chicago in 1934, it makes sense that Roche would have been updated
by them on developments occurring in Ireland at that time, because by the
late 1930s Roche had discontinued the use of metal taps for his dancers,
and the use of taps was strictly forbidden in the all the feiseanna sponsored by the Harp and Shamrock Club. The list of rules for the 1951 Feis
clearly states this prohibition.

Until the late 1950s, dancers in Chicago continued to wear only hard-
soled shoes no matter what type of dance they performed, whether the
jig, reel, slip jig, hornpipe, set dance, or figure dances. [Fig. 83] Today's
dancers might be surprised by this fact, since presently females wear a

balletic pump for "light" dances such as the reel or slip jig, and for most figure dances.[9] Males, too, wear a lighter, soft-sole oxford-style shoe for the reel, similar to a jazz shoe. Even though this switch in footwear did not occur in Chicago until the late 1950s, according to John Cullinane, some female dancers in Ireland were wearing a ballet shoe for some dances as early as 1924.[10] Currently, hard shoes worn by Irish dancers use a fiberglass tip in order to get a good sound. Shoe innovations are typically scrutinized by the Irish Dancing Commission and exact shoe design guidelines are established.

Costumes

Over the decades, there have been considerable changes in the costumes worn by Chicago dancers, particularly for females. For the most part, males continued to wear long dark pants, a white shirt, and a cummerbund or sash of some kind around the waist. There were some exceptions to this. For instance, in the *Feis of King Guaire,* the production staged in 1910, some of the boys wore costumes reminiscent of the medieval period, while others wore attire with an almost nautical flavor—a sailor-type beret on the head, knee britches or knickers, and a wide-collar shirt. [Fig. 11] These types of costumes were not typically worn by the dancers, but were created specifically for this production. Young dancers who performed in the *Feis of King Guaire* continued to wear those costumes for other dance events for several years after. Knee-length trousers were worn by male dancers in Ireland, and both the photo of McNamara, Ryan, and Coleman (on the front cover of this book) and a photo of William Ferry, who danced in Chicago in 1920, show the dancers wearing these. [Figs. 8, 21]

When Pat Roche appeared at the Irish Village, he wore long trousers, a white shirt, and a cummerbund. [Fig. 24] The front of the shirt had a cluster of shamrocks embroidered on one side and a harp embroidered on the other side. His cummerbund also had embroidery on it. Kilts were never worn by male dancers in Chicago until the 1960s. Donal O'Connor, the Gaelic League representative who came to Chicago to organize the *feiseanna* in 1912 and 1913, is pictured wearing a kilt, however, it must be remembered that he was not a dancer. [Fig. 17] Avid members of the Gaelic League wore kilts, so it was not surprising for him to be pictured in this style of dress. In Chicago, kilts continued to be worn by male

COURTESY THE DENNEHY FAMILY

84. Dennehy Dancers, 1970s: Kathy Crowe,
Dominic Byrne, Arlene Kirwin, Brian McCormick.

dancers from the early 1960s until the late 1990s. [Fig. 84] Even though some young male dancers balked at the idea of having to wear a kilt, and some young men refused to partake in Irish dancing because of this fact, the kilt was an understood requirement for competitive male dancers until the late 1990s. With the influence of *Riverdance,* trousers have once again become the preferred garb for male competitive dancers.

The females' costumes saw much more variation. At the beginning of the twentieth century, the common attire was a white dress with a green sash either going around the waist or going over one shoulder and ending at the waist. [Fig. 13] In those early days, the one exception for the women was in the production of the *Feis of King Guaire.* Just as with the males, the females' costumes for that event were medieval in style. The dress was mid-calf length with a heavy cape over the dress. [Figs. 9-10] John Cullinane explains that a hooded cloak worn over a white dress was

142

a very popular costume throughout Ireland at the start of the last century, but became outdated toward the end of the 1920s.[11] Except for this one aberration, the females' costumes remained very simple. One young dancer who appeared at an event in 1918 is pictured in a simple white dress with shamrocks on the bodice. [Fig. 18] A written description that appeared in a 1918 article, also indicates that the costumes were quite simple: "Dressed in pretty green costumes the girls attracted a big crowd."[12]

The dancers who appeared at the Irish Village in 1934 wore a variety of costumes. Roche's young female dancers were outfitted in a dress consisting of a green skirt, white short-sleeved bodice, and a black vest laced up the front. [Fig. 27] A photograph of Mae Kennedy Kane shows her in a dress, most likely green in color, which had one large shamrock covering the entire bodice. The material appears to be taffeta or satin. [Fig. 25] The two young dancers, Kathleen Winkler and Loretta Mungovan, who appeared at the Irish Village wore costumes that most resembled those being worn by dancers in Ireland at that time: a white dress with a pleated skirt and coatee (a waist-length jacket with long sleeves) worn over the dress. A shawl, hung from one shoulder, was attached at the waist on the opposite side, and was the length of the dress. [Fig. 29] Violet Danaher, the dancer from Ireland who was featured at the Irish Village, wore a similar costume. [Fig. 22]

During the years 1930-60, Roche's costumes changed several times. There were satin blouses with satin pleated skirts and a shawl. [Fig. 47] Another costume consisted of a pleated skirt with a suit jacket buttoned up to the neck, a collar around the neckline, and a shawl fastened at one shoulder with a Tara brooch. [Fig. 83] Evidently, the suit jackets varied in color—green, blue, or black, depending on which of his various classes the dancers were enrolled. According to both Lucille McKillop and Mary Shevlin McNamara, Roche became interested in blue as a color option when he learned that blue had been the traditional color for Ireland.[13] Following the suit jacket costumes, there were green wool, long-sleeved dresses with a cord tied around the waist and a shawl attached at both shoulders with Tara brooches. Another costume for younger dancers consisted of a satin pleated skirt and a satin vest over a white blouse. A popular Roche costume in the late 1950s consisted of a white pleated skirt, a white blouse with puffy sleeves, a green velvet vest laced up the front, and an orange shawl fastened at one shoulder. [Fig. 58] The dancers wore black ankle socks with this outfit. The final costume that Pat Roche's dancers wore was a white dress with a pleated skirt, a green wool vest, a burnt orange cummerbund, and a white embroidered shawl.[14] [Fig. 59] Black tights were worn with these costumes.

The Roche dancers who opened their own schools in the late 1940s used variations on the theme of pleated skirts, long-sleeved jackets, and a shawl for their class costumes. The color combinations varied, but the basic colors continued to be green, white, gold, and black. Plaids were incorporated in costumes by Mary Campbell and Frank Culhane. [Fig. 61] At one point, in the early 1950s, Jim Shea's dancers wore a white tam as part of their costume. [Fig. 56] Mary Shevlin McNamara's first costumes were very similar to the type worn by Roche's dancers at the Irish Village. Shevlin's dancers wore green skirts, white short-sleeve blouses, and black vest, but they also had a plaid shawl. [Fig. 57] All of these teachers changed their costumes in later years. For instance, Mary Campbell switched to a black skirt and white jacket, but in 1953, they wore the costumes described above. [Fig. 85]

When Marge Bartishell opened her school in the late 1950s, her costumes were unique in that they were light blue in color. It consisted of a white dress with a pleated skirt over which was a light blue jacket. An embroidered white shawl completed the ensemble. In later years the Dennehy dancers wore white embroidered dresses with blue accents. [Fig. 54] At yet another point they wore dark blue embroidered dresses. [Fig. 84] The Dennehy dancers continue to use blue as the distinctive color for their class costumes.

In addition to class costumes, students now purchase solo costumes worn for the advanced grades and championships in competitions. The costumes have become much more ornate and theatrical over the years. Sequins, metallic threads, rhinestones, and even feathers are used to decorate solo costumes. As expected, with the more ornate style has come a bigger price tag for each costume. Even though this is somewhat of a concern among Irish dancing teachers, it is difficult to change the trend. An industry has developed for the design and construction of these costumes, so changing the status quo is complicated. Additionally, many parents are

85. Mary Campbell's Dancers performing at Shuberts Field, 1950s.

willing to pay an extraordinary amount for a solo costume if they feel it will give their dancer an extra advantage.

Hair Styles

Hair styles for dancers have also changed over the years. Up until the late 1980s, dancers wore a varietiey of styles based on the type of hair they had, and the length they desired. There were always some Irish dancers who had curly hair and wore ringlets for dancing events. However, most dancers had straight hair and wore it that way for both competition and exhibition. In the late 1980s dancing schools started requiring curls. Parents were given lessons on the correct curling techniques, and dancers could be seen with pink sponge curlers covering their heads as they prepared for their competition. This was a time-consuming technique for styling the hair. Once curly wigs were introduced as way to eliminate the hours of setting and styling, teachers and parents alike endorsed the wigs as a solution. Now most Irish dancers wear wigs. Even though there is still discussion on the matter, the wigs seem to have become (to the dismay of many) part of the accepted look or image of an Irish dancer.[15]

Posture

Another feature of an Irish dancer's appearance is the position of the arms. During the 1940s onward, for competitive dancing in Chicago, arms were always held straight down and pinned to the sides. Interestingly, in the early photographs of Chicago dancers they are pictured with hands on their hips. Even the picture of some of the dancers who performed at the Century of Progress in 1934 shows them with their hands on their hips. These images are identical to an Ulster Museum photograph of Cassie O'Neill dancing in the 1904 Glenarm Feis in Co. Antrim that shows her with her hands on her hips. John Cullinane cites several examples of dancing with hands on the hips. He also points out that dancing with hands on the hips was done by women in Cork up to the late 1950s. Cullinane concludes that:

> These and many other examples (not listed) serve to show that in much of our older dances hand movements were not only permitted but were frequently a necessary part of the dance. In conclusion then we must keep in mind the fact that the present rigid positioning of the hand is of recent introduction.[16]

Before seeing the photos of the Chicago dancers, the positioning of the hands on the hips was considered a caricature of Irish dancers, typical of the stage Irishman popular during vaudeville and preserved by Broadway and Hollywood. But, as shown, research indicates that it was indeed a style popular in certain sections of Ireland. As the dancing styles became more standardized with the creation of the Irish Dancing Commission in Ireland in 1931, and with the increased emphasis on competitive dancing, variations in style have diminished and standardization has become the rule in dancing posture, shoe construction, and costume style.

Notes

Introduction

1. Lawrence J. McCaffrey, *The Irish Diaspora in America* (Bloomington: Indiana Univ. Press, 1976), 6.

2. Ibid.

3. Joseph P. O'Grady, *How the Irish Became Americans* (Boston: Twayne, 1973), 113.

4. Andrew Greeley, *The Irish Americans: The Rise to Money and Power* (New York: Harper, 1981), 78.

5. Ibid.

6. Francis O'Neill, *Irish Folk Music: A Fascinating Hobby* (Chicago: Regan, 1910); and *Irish Minstrels and Musicians* (Chicago: Regan, 1913). The only other studies of Irish music and dance in Chicago are Lawrence McCullough, *Irish Music in Chicago* (Ph.D. diss., Univ. of Pittsburgh, 1978); and "The Role of Language, Music, and Dance in the Revival of Irish Culture in Chicago, Illinois," *Ethnicity* 7 (1980): 436-44. A literature on Irish dance in general is a contemporary phenomenon. The first Ph.D. dissertation on Irish dance was written only in 1988: Catherine E. Foley, *Irish Traditional Step Dance in North Kerry* (Ph.D. diss., Laban Centre/Univ. of London, 1988). The first essay to appear in an academic journal appeared only in 1995: Moe Meyer, "The Politics of Orality: A Study of the Irish *Scoil Rince*," *Dance Research Journal* 27.1 (Spring 1995): 25-39.

Chapter One

1. Typical of these is a description of Dan O'Keefe, a late nineteenth-century saloon owner: "though not specially distinguished as a piper, competent authorities allow that O'Keefe was an exceptionally fine dancer" (O'Neill, *Irish Minstrels and Musicians,* 349).

2. Neil Harris, "Selling Culture at the World's Columbian Exposition," in *Imagining an Irish Past: The Celtic Revival, 1840-1940*, ed. T. J. Edelstein (Chicago: Chicago Univ. Press, 1992), 90.

3. Ibid., 95.

4. Eileen Durkin, "Saint Patrick's Day at Saint Patrick's Church," in *At the Crossroads: Old Saint Patrick's and the Chicago Irish*, ed. Ellen Skerrett (Chicago: Wild Onion, 1997), 3.

5. Ibid., 1-2.

6. Ibid.

7. R. V. Comerford, "Nation, Nationalism, and the Irish Language," in *Perspectives on Irish Nationalism*, eds. Thomas E. Hachey and Lawrence J. McCaffrey (Lexington: Univ. Press of Kentucky, 1989), 35.

8. In the regard see also Breandan Breathnach, *Dancing In Ireland* (Miltown-Malbay: Dal gCais, 1983), 50; Elizabeth Malcolm, "Popular Recreation in Nineteenth-Century Ireland," in *Irish Culture and Nationalism, 1750-1950*, eds. Olivier MacDonagh, W. F. Mandle and Pauric Travers (New York: St. Martin's, 1983), 49-50; and Meyer, "Politics of Orality," 30.

9. John P. Cullinane, *Further Aspects of the History of Irish Dancing* (Cork: Cullinane, 1990), 37.

10. Timothy G. McMahon, *Grand Opportunity: The Gaelic Revival and Irish Society, 1893-1910* (Syracuse: Syracuse UP, 2008), 155-186.

11. O'Neill, *Irish Folk Music*, 44.

12. Ibid.

13. John Ennis, "Irish Music Club Annual Festival," *Citizen* 04 July 1903, 6.

14. McMahon, *Grand Opportunity*, 173-74.

15. O'Neill, *Irish Minstrels*, 23.

16. Ibid., 281.

17. Ibid., 422.

18. "Irish Dancing," *Citizen* 16 January 1904, 7.

19. Alice Ryan O'Connor, personal interview, 04 January 2008.

20. John Ennis, "Hugh O'Neill, Ireland's Champion Dancer," *Citizen* 03 December 1904, 3.

21. "Irish Music," *Citizen* 14 October 1905, 5.

22. "Irish Dancing Club," *Citizen*, 22 September 1906, 7.

23. Ibid.

24. "The Gaelic Society," *Citizen* 22 February 1908, 7.

25. "Irish Music Club to Dance," *Citizen* 10 October 1908, 5.

26. "Irish Club Elects Officers," *Citizen* 14 July 1906, 7.

27. John Cullinane, *Aspects of the History of Irish Dancing* (Cork: Cullinane, 1999), 28.

28. "United Irish Societies Picnic," *Citizen*, 21 August 1909, 1. The high standard of dancing of a five-year old, Margaret Meagher, was singled out for special praise, demonstrating the growing participation of children in Irish dance.

Chapter Two

1. Thomas O'Shaughnessy, "The Feis of King Guaire," *Sunday Record Herald* 22 May 1910.

2. Ibid.

3. Ibid.

4. Ibid.

5. "Chicago Gaels to Hold a 'Feis,'" *Chicago Daily Tribune* 30 April 1911, 13. Douglas Hyde was the founder of the Gaelic League.

6. Ibid.

7. "Dedication Emmet Memorial Hall," *Citizen* 14 October 1911, 1.

8. "United Irish Societies," *Citizen* 20 August 1910, 1. A photo of Coleman, Ryan, and McNamara appears on the front cover of this book.

9. Ibid.

10. Ibid.

11. "Entertainment and Ball," *Citizen* April 1912.

12. "National Irish 'Feis' to be Held at Gaelic Park Today," *Chicago Daily Tribune* 28 July 1912, A6.

13. Ibid.

14. "About Irish Dancing," *Citizen* 29 June 1912, 6.

15. "Never in the History of Chicago," *Citizen* 03 August 1912, 8.

16. "Stage Irishmen Barred at Feis," *Chicago Daily Tribune* 29 July 1912, 5.

17. Ibid.

18. Ibid.

19. "Never in the History of Chicago, *Citizen* 03 August 1912, 8.

20. "Gaelic Junior Dancing and Choral Clubs," *Citizen* 26 October 1912, 3.

21. "Gaelic Junior Dancing and Choral Clubs," *Citizen* 11 January 1913, 8.

22. "Gaelic Dancing Association," *Citizen* 25 January 1913, 7.

23. "United Gaelic Clubs of Chicago," *Citizen* 15 March 1913, 5.

24. Mary Philben, "Gaelic Dancing Association," *Citizen* 28 June 1913, 5.

25. Ibid.

26. Ibid.

27. "Gaelic League Plans Revival of the Tara Feis," 14 June 1913, 5.

28. "Feis, Ancient Irish Fete," *Chicago Daily Tribune* 20 July 1913, B6.

29. "Chicago Festival Draws Big Crowd," *Chicago Daily Tribune* 04 August 1913.

30. "Irish Feis Promises To Be a Big Success," *Citizen* 02 August 1913, 6.

31. There were a few articles in the *Tribune* that reported that the United Irish Societies of Chicago held picnics in 1914 and 1915 that featured Irish dancing contests. The gatherings were held to commemorate the Battle of Yellow Ford and Lady Day in Harvest. The only dancer who was identified was Agnes Daley who was credited as being a "champion Irish dancer of this country" ("5,000 Volunteer for Irish Fight," *Chicago Daily Tribune* 10 August 1914, 7).

32. "Classy Exhibition of Irish Step Dancing," *Citizen* 31 August 1917, 8.

33. "United Celtic American Societies," *Citizen* 05 July 1918. The selection of adjudicators was a major issue in the early days of competitions, both in the U.S. and Ireland. In this regard see also: Frank Hall, *Competitive Irish Dance: Art, Sport Duty* (Madison: Macater Press, 2008), 36-38.

34. "Gaelic Park Open," *Citizen* 24 May 1918, 2.

35. "United Celtic American Societies," *Citizen* 05 July 1918, 5.

36. "McNamara's Big Day at Gaelic Park," *Citizen* 25 July 1919, 3.

37. "Professor McNamara's Dancers Give Annual Entertainment," *Citizen* 04 March 1921.

38. Whether to include set dancing in competitions, indeed whether to include set dancing in Irish dancing at all was a contentious and hotly debated issue in Ireland and the Gaelic League. Hardline nationalists would not accept set dancing as a legitimate national form. In this regard, see also: Hall, *Competitive Irish Dance*, 11, 30-35; and Cormac Mac Fhionnlaoich, *Stair na Rincí Gaelacha* (Atha Cliath: AnnCoimisiún le Rincí Gaelacha, 1973), 7-8.

39. James J. Mahoney, "Gaelic Park Athletic News," *Citizen* 27 June 1919, 6.

40. "Entertainment on St. Patrick's Day Eve," *Citizen* 12 March 1920, 3.

41. Ibid.

42. This switch from nationalism to religion parallels and is contemporaneous with the "Irish Ireland" movement in Ireland. See Terence Brown, *Ireland: A Social and Cultural History, 1922 to the Present* (Ithaca: Cornell Univ. Press, 1985), 37-61.

43. "Ireland's Days at Gaelic Park," *Southtown Economist* 02 September 1925, 6.

44. "Pupils of Miss Margaret Hayes to Dance for United Irish Societies," *Southtown Economist* 14 August 1926.

45. "Miss E. Burchenal Lauds Irish Dancing," *Citizen* 31 July 1926, 6. See also Elizabeth Burchenal, *Rince Na Eirann* (New York: Barnes, 1924).

46. "Professor John McNamara is Mourned by Many People," *New World* 08 February 1929.

47. With the creation of Irish Free State, the Gaelic League even in Ireland lost eighty-five percent of its membership literally overnight. In this regard, see Brown, *Ireland*, 43.

48. Charles Fanning, Ellen Skerrett and John Corrigan, *Nineteenth Century Irish: A Social and Political Portrait* (Chicago: Loyola Univ. Press), 21.

Chapter Three

1. "Irish Artists Here for Part in Fair's Irish Village Event," *New World* 08 June 1934, 7.

2. Pat Roche, personal interview, 25 July 1994.

3. "Irish Village Heeds Warning," *New World* 06 July 1934, 2.

4. "Century of Progress Brevities," *Chicago Tribune* 03 July 1934, 7.

5. Roche, personal interview, 04 April 1995.

6. Mick Moloney, "The History of Céilí Bands in America" (paper presented at the Comhaltas National Convention, Chicago, 09 April 1994).

7. Roche, personal interview, 25 July 1994,

8. Kate Bell Downs, personal interview, 22 July 1994.

9. Roche, personal interview, 25 July 1994.

10. Ibid., 08 April 1994.

11. "Irish Take Over the Fair Today; Expect 100,000," *Chicago Tribune* 15 August 1934.

12. "Interesting Historical Facts Brought to Chicago's Midst by New Century of Progress," *New World* 08 June 1934, 7.

13. "Design Costumes in Erin for Chicago's Pageant of Ireland," *New World* 06 July 1934, 3.

14. Roche, personal interview, 25 July 1994.

15. "'Pageant of the Celt' to Tell History of Irish Peoples," *Chicago Tribune* 26 August 1934, 12.

16. "Old Irish Glory Thrills Throng at Celt Pageant," *Chicago Tribune* 29 August 1934.

17. Nancy O'Malley Scoville, personal interview, 14 September 1994.

18. "West Side Irish Take Labor Day Excursion," *Garfieldian* 29 August 1935, 6.

19. "Irish Parade Moves West Siders' Hearts," *Garfieldian* 19 March 1952, 3G.

20. Arthur Flynn, *Irish Dance* (Dublin: Folens, n.d.), 94. See also Alan Gailey, *Irish Folk Drama* (Cork: Mercier, 1969).

21. "Irish Dancers Will Stage a 'Night in Erin,'" *Garfieldian* 28 July 1938.

22. "Planning That Big Day for the Irish," *Garfieldian* 11 March 1948, 14.

23. "Pipers Did Pipe and Steppers Did Step," *Lakeview Booster* 17 March 1946.

24. "Harp Shamrock Club on Boat Trip," *Garfieldian* 23 June 1938, 5.

25. Lucille McKillop and Rosalina McKillop, personal interview, 04 January 1995.

26. Roche, personal interview, 25 July 1994.

27. Cullinane, *Further Aspects of the History of Irish Dancing,* 72.

28. "Sixth Annual 'Holy Hill' Pilgrimage Conducted by Pat Roche on Sunday, September 17," *American Gael* September 1939.

29. "Program of Gaelic Dancing To Be Given," *Garfieldian* 03 January 1935, 2.

30. Ann Dillon Quinn, personal correspondence, 07 February 1995.

31. Kate Bell Downs and Loretto Schaar Kistinger, personal interview, 15 September 1994.

32. "Many Irish Parties Set for Friday," *Garfieldian* 16 March 1950, 1.

33. "Benefit Dance Big Success," *American Gael* April 1940.

34. "Gaelic Festival at Mills Park This Saturday," *Garfieldian* 19 August 1937, 1.

35. "Gaelic Festival Held Over Until Saturday," *Garfieldian* 28 August 1937, 1.

36. "Two Speakers Will Address Irish Day Fete," *Garfieldian* 09 August 1945.

37. For an interesting discussion of McKenna and his stature in New York City, and hence the significance of the Roche dancers' competitive win over the McKenna dancers, see Mick Moloney and Orfhlaith Ní Bhriain, "Changes in Irish Dance in New York over the Past Half-Century," in *Close to the Floor: Irish Dance From the Boreen to Broadway*, eds. Mick Moloney, J'aime Morrison, and Colin Quigley (Madison: Macater, 2008), 109-114.

38. Catherine E. Foley, "Stepping Out of History: The Origins and Development of Traditional Irish Dance" (paper presented at the Irish American Cultural Institute, Chicago, 05 April 1995).

39. "Irish Ready for Two Big Picnics Thursday," *Garfieldian* 08 August 1946, 13.

40. Roche, personal interview, 08 April 1994.

41. Ibid., 19 October 1993.

42. "Irish Celebrate Lady Day Monday at Pilsen Park," *Garfieldian* 11 August 1949, 11.

43. "Irish Girls Step Out at 'Tostal,'" *Southtown Economist* August 1950.

44. "Postpone Feis Until Saturday," *Garfieldian* 25 June 1952, 1.

45. Roche, personal interview, 19 October 1993.

Chapter Four

1. John P. Cullinane, *Aspects of the History of Irish Dancing in North America* (Cork: Cullinane, 1997), 79.

2. This dramatic shift in dancing styles and its effect on dancing schools is discussed in Moloney and Ní Bhriain, "Changes in Irish Dance in New York," 108-19.

3. Dennis Dennehy, personal interview, 04 January 1995.

4. Cullinane, *Irish Dancing in North America,* 80.

5. Dennehy, personal interview, 14 September 2007.

6. Jim Shea, personal interview, 04 January 1995.

7. Mary Campbell, personal interview, 04 January 1995.

8. In addition to playing drums, Patrick Gilhooley was also in several dances.

9. Lawrence McCullough, *Irish Music in Chicago: An Ethnomusicological Study* (Ph.D. diss., Univ. of Pittsburgh, 1978), 48.

10. Dennehy, personal interview, 14 September 2007.

11. Ibid.

12. "Begorra! Sure and Irish Is Up in Harvey Area," *Chicago Tribune* 22 September 1963, SW2.

13. "400 Children to Take Part in Irish Feis," *Chicago Tribune* 02 February 1964, SW6.

14. "Irish Club to Hold Culture Festival Today," *Chicago Tribune* 05 June 1966, 7.

15. Nora Harling Gardner, personal interview, 03 March 2007.

16. John P. Cullinane, *An Coimisiun le Rinci Gaelacha: Its Origins and Evolution* (Cork: Cullinane, 2003), 87.

17. In this regard, see Frank Hall's discussion of the organizational split in *Competitive Irish Dance*, 38-40.

18. Two out-of-towners also sat for the teacher's exam in Chicago in 1976. Kate Flanagan, the author of this book, came from Winona, Minnesota; and David Meyer, the editor of this book, came from Milwaukee.

19. Dennehy, personal interview, 14 September 2007.

20. John P. Cullinane, *Aspects of the History of Irish Ceili Dancing,* 1897-1997 (Cork: Cullinane, 1998), 13.

21. "Meet Noel Rice, Irish Musician of the Francis O'Neill Club," *Irish American News* October 1977, 2.

22. "To Teach Native Irish Dancing," *Irish American News* December 1977, 9; and "IMA to Hold Regular Ceilis," *Irish American News* October 1977, 23.

23. "1000 Step Dancers in Chicago Feis," *Irish American News* August 1977, 3.

24. Mike and Agnes Howard, personal interview, 28 April 2007. Mike and Agnes are the parents of Mark Howard, Director of the famed Trinity Academy.

25. "Chicagoans Win at Pre-Feis Dance," *Irish American News* August 1980, 18-19.

26. Michael Flatley, *Lord of the Dance* (New York: Simon, 2006), 46.

27. "The Annual Midwest Feis That Was," *Irish American News* August 1979, 23-24.

28. Oireachtas Features Best in Midwest," *Irish American News* August 1981, 21.

29. "Midwest Fleadh Cheoil - A Day of Winners," *Irish American News* May 1980, 4.

30. "Irish Family Night August 15," *Irish American News* June 1977.

31. "August 15 Named Irish Day by Mayor," *Irish American News* August 1977.

32. "Three Big Shows at Irish Family Day," *Irish American News* August 1978, 3.

33. "Folk Festival Set for August 27," *Irish American News* June 1977; and "Irish at Cultural Center," *Irish American News* May 1980, 2.

Chapter Five

1. Sid Smith, "Lord of the Glitz," *Chicago Tribune* 05 April 1997, 23.

2. In fact, the term "riverdancing" has become part of dance vocabulary, much to the surprise of many veteran Irish dance teachers, who are often asked, "Do you teach riverdancing?"

3. Patrick Pacheco, "From Chieftains to Dance 'Lord," *Los Angeles Times* 23 March 1997, F12.

4. Kieran Jordan, "Lord of the Dance: Preview and Interview," *Boston Irish Reporter* April 1997, 18.

5. David Dougill, "Ceili Caper," *Sunday Times* 21 July 1996, 10.21

6. Lynn Voedisch, "Dance Review," *Chicago Sun-Times* 07 April 1997, 30.

7. Claudia LaRocco, "Irish Eyes Are Burning Bright, Irish Feet Are Stepping Light," *New York Times* 29 September 2005 <http://www.nytimes.com/2005/09/29/arts/dance/29flat.html>

8. Janice Steinberg, "Michael Flatley Draws Kudos and Brickbats in Equal Amount," *Union Tribune* 27 October 2005 <http://www.signonsandiego.com/news/features/20051027-9999-1w27flatley1.html>

9. Ibid.

10. Ibid.

11. Ibid.

12. Paul Martin, "Flatley Is World's Top Earner," *Irish Daily Mirror,* reported on <http://michaelflatley.com>. See also "Well Heeled; Flatley taps into a fortune to be Ireland's top earner," *Sunday Mirror* 18 February 2001 <http://findarticles.com/p/articles/mi_qn4161/is_20010218/ai_n14523631>

13. Jim Distasio, "Breaking Tradition Trinity Pushes Irish Dance to New Levels," *Daily Herald* [Arlington Heights, Ill.] 21 November 2003, 11.

14. Michelle Rounder, "The Trinity Legacy Revealed—Laying Down the Thunder," *Irish Dancing Magazine* <http://www.trinitydancers.com/article2.shtml>

15. Michael Rydznski, "Irish Trinity Dance, Whose Works Predate Riverdance, Came About 'By Accident," *Irvine World News* 06 March 2003 <http://www.irvineworldnews.com/Bstories/mar6/trinity.html>

16. Rounder, "Trinity Legacy Revealed."

17. Jennifer Dunning, "The Irish Way with Flying Feet and a Champion or Two," *New York Times* 14 August 1997, C13.

18. Molly McQuade, "Trinity Irish Dance Company," *Dance Magazine* November 1997, 11.

19. M.S. Mason, "Ethnic Dance Ensembles Kick Up a Storm," *Christian Science Monitor* 13 August 1999, 19.

20. Ibid.

21. Cullinane, *Aspects of the History of Irish Dancing,* 11.

22. Ibid., 12-13.

23. Gearóid Ó hAllmhuráin, *Irish Traditional Music* (Dublin: O'Brien, 1998), 57.

24. Brennan, *Story of Irish Dance,* 22.

25. Ibid., 31. See also Hall, *Competitive Irish Dance,* 27-41.

26. McKillop, personal interview.

27. Breathnach, *Dancing in Ireland,* 23-26, 41-42; and Hall, *Competitive Irish Dance,* 20-23.

28. Jack Anderson, "Bodies Rigid, as the Feet Put on a Show," *New York Times* 21 March 2000, E5.

29. Tobi Tobias, "Celtics Win," *New York Magazine* 03 April 2000, 78.

30. Breandan Breathnach, *Folk Music and Dances of Ireland* (Cork: Mercier 1977), 42.

31. Martha Ullman West, "One Step Beyond, Trinity Irish Dance," *Dance Magazine* June 2001, 78.

32. Jack Anderson, "Dancing Up a Cheerful Storm," *New York Times* 01 March 2002, E1:4.

33. Jennie Schulman, "Trinity Irish Dance Company Steps onto the Joyce Stage," *Backstage* 22 March 2002, 11.

34. Ibid.

35. Tom Strini, "Trinity Too Much of a Good Thing: Flawless Delivery of New, Traditional Work," *Milwaukee Journal Sentinel* 10 October 2004, 7.

Appendices

1. Cullinane, *Aspects of the History of Irish Dancing* 6.

2. Ibid., 7.

3. Breathnach, *Folk Music and Dances of Ireland,* 43.

4. Ibid., 49.

5. Ibid., 53.

6. Cullinane, *Aspects of the History of Irish Dancing,* 68.

7. Downs, personal interview, 22 July 1994.

8. Roche, personal interview, 17 October 1992; and 19 October 1993.

9. In fact, Irish dances now fall into two classifications based on the type of shoe worn: light dances, or soft-shoe dances (which are performed in soft-soled pumps) and heavy dances, or hard-shoe dances (which are performed in hard-soled shoes).

10. Cullinane, *Aspects of the History of Irish Dancing,* 68.

11. Ibid., 63.

12. "Gaelic Park Open," *Citizen* 24 May 1918, 2.

13. McNamara and McKillop, personal interview, 03 January 1995; and 04 January 1995.

14. There were also dark blue vests and red cummerbunds that could be worn interchangeably. Only a few dancers had the extra blue and red combination and they were not worn on many occasions.

15. The use of wigs as part of Irish dancing costume is still a heated debate. In fact the debate itself has become known as the "wig controversy". See Brennan, *Story of Irish Dance,* 157-58. In 2008, a motion was entered at the annual meeting of the IDTANA requesting a ban on wigs in North America. The membership refused to vote on the motion.

16. Cullinane, *Aspects of the History of Irish Dancing,* 71. Some would debate Cullinane's assertion that arms held at the sides is of recent introduction; in this regard see Hall, *Competitive Irish Dance,* 13-25. Hall identifies this posture as originating with the famed 18th-c. Irish Dancing Masters.

Index

Lightning Source Inc.
LaVergne, TN USA
14 August 2009
154870LV00005B/2/P